THE AMERICAN FLY TYER'S HANDBOOK

THE AMERICAN FLY TYER'S HANDBOOK

edited by
KENNETH E. BAY

Winchester Press

Copyright © 1979 by Kenneth E. Bay

All rights reserved

Library of Congress Cataloging in Publication Data
Main entry under title:

The American fly tyer's handbook.

  Includes index.
  1. Fly tying. I. Bay, Kenneth E., 1920-
SH451.A46   688.7'8   78-31584
ISBN 0-87691-287-0

9 8 7 6 5 4 3 2 1

Published by Winchester Press
205 East 42nd Street
New York, N.Y. 10017

WINCHESTER is a Trademark of Olin Corporation used by
Winchester Press, Inc. under authority and control of the
Trademark Proprietor

Printed in the United States of America

Introduction

This is a book of fly-tying instruction by fifteen master fly tyers from different parts of the country. For the most part, the talents of these men have never before appeared in print. Some are already legendary by reputation but have been observed in action only by a small number of tyers and fishermen.

Each section of this book is the personal handiwork of the individual tyer named. Each presents instructions and helpful hints for tying a favorite fly, chosen for its fish-taking effectiveness and fly-tying complexity. The hands in the photos are the fly tyer's and the comments and captions are in his own words. Only minor editing has been done.

Assembling such a manuscript can be a monumental task, considering that procedures and deadlines were imposed on fifteen different individuals. However, ever since I started to contact the contributors about two years ago, I have been the happy recipient of such enthusiasm and cooperation that my task has been pleasurable — which has to be the primary reward for writing or editing a book on a fishing subject. All of these gentlemen have my heartfelt thanks for making this book possible. Hopefully, they will reap some rewards from their exposure.

My main joy in fly tying has always been helping those of lesser experience. With two earlier volumes on basic fly tying behind me, I consider this one to be the culmination of that desire. I hope you will enjoy the book, as well as learn from the talent represented between these covers.

Kenneth E. Bay
Nyack, N.Y.

Contents

1 Burr's Brite *(Walter E. Burr)*   1
2 Ted's Crayfish *(Theodore J. Godfrey)*   5
3 The Matuka Sculpin *(Edward Graham)*   11
4 The Pre-Emerger Nymph *(Hal W. Janssen)*   19
5 The Cotton-Thread Stonefly Nymph *(Charles Krom)*   25
6 The Emergent Caddis Pupa *(Gary LaFontaine)*   33
7 The Robber Fly *(Chauncey K. Lively)*   41
8 The Two-Feather May *(John F. McKim)*   47
9 The Marabou Dragon Nymph *(John Merwin)*   55
10 The Flat-Wing Fly *(Sid A. Neff, Jr.)*   65
11 The Adult Stone Fly *(Ted Niemeyer)*   75
12 The Hair-Wing Matuka *(Eric W. Peper)*   85
13 Vinny's Midge *(John Shollenberger)*   93
14 The Cardinelle *(Dick Surette)*   101
15 The Painted Lady *(Ralph Wahl)*   105
    Authors' Biographies   113
    Index   119

Burr's Brite
By WALTER E. BURR
Photographs by Wilson B. Scofield

This fan-wing pattern was submitted to the United Fly Tyers in the late sixties and was named Burr's Brite by the editor of the UFT *Round Table*. It is most effective during the periods dawn to sunrise and sunset to dark. At these times, the ultraviolet rays maximize and cause the green fluorescent wool body to glow like the natural fly body. If the pattern size is matched to the natural, the fish will take this fly regardless of the natural on the water.

The fan-wing dry fly has the advantage of greater visibility and added delicacy of presentation. Its disadvantage is the tendency to spin, causing the leader to twist. Therefore, in tying the fly, it is better to have the wings on the small, rather than having them on the large, side.

Wings should be sized so that their height will be one to one and a half times that of the hook shank length, measured from behind the eye to the bend. Sizing is accomplished by removing the necessary fibers adjacent to the butt on either side of the stem of the duck breast feather. Each step in the tying procedures should be secured with a single half hitch.

MATERIALS

TAIL: white polar bear guard hairs or fibers stripped from a hackle
WINGS: mallard duck breast feathers
BODY: green fluorescent wool
HOOK: Mustad #94833, size 12

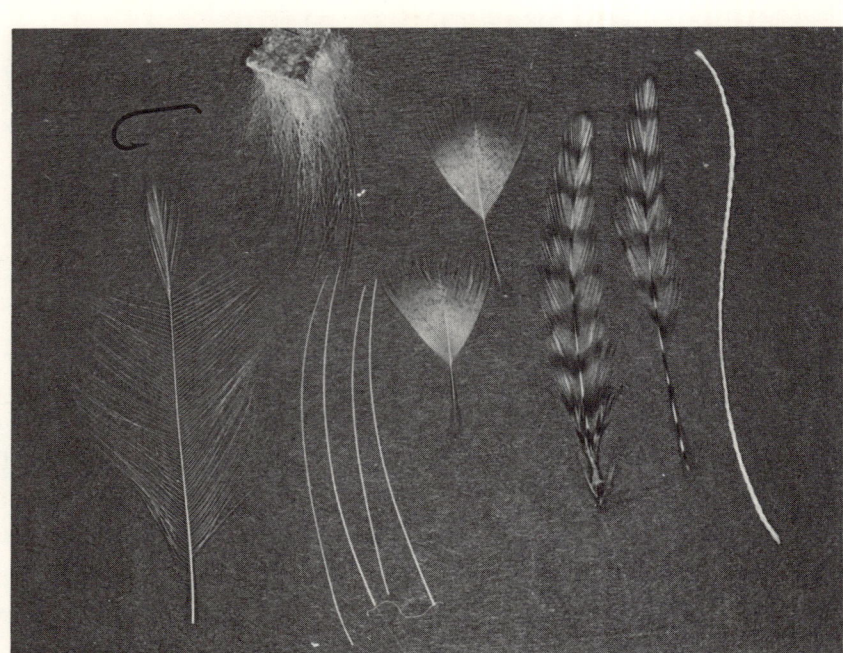

1
The materials for the Burr's Brite fan-wing dry fly.

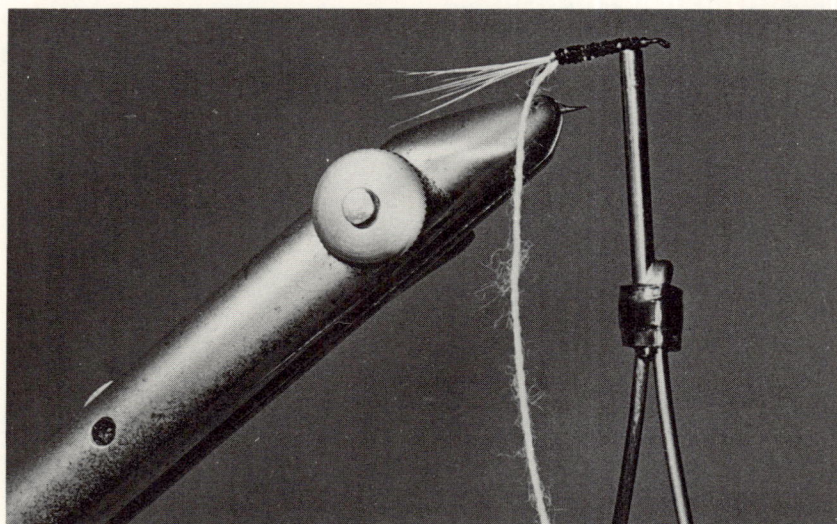

2
Tie in the tail fibers at the bend of the hook. The tips of the tail fibers should extend beyond the hook bend for a length equal to the hook shank (from behind the eye to the bend). Tie in the body material at the bend of the hook.

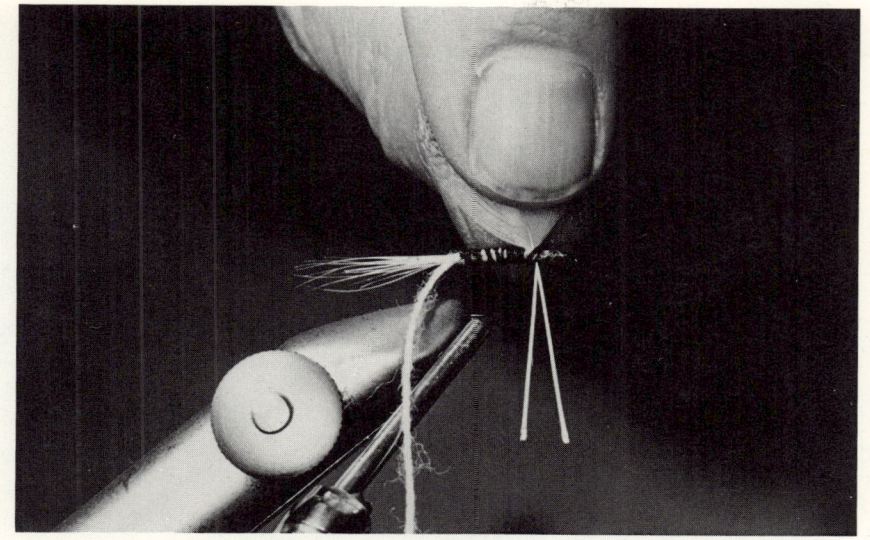

3

With the left thumb and forefinger, grasp the matched wing tips, with the convex sides together, and place the wings on the hook shank one-third of the distance behind the eye so that the base wing fibers are at the shank and the shank splits the wing stems. Make four to five turns of thread.

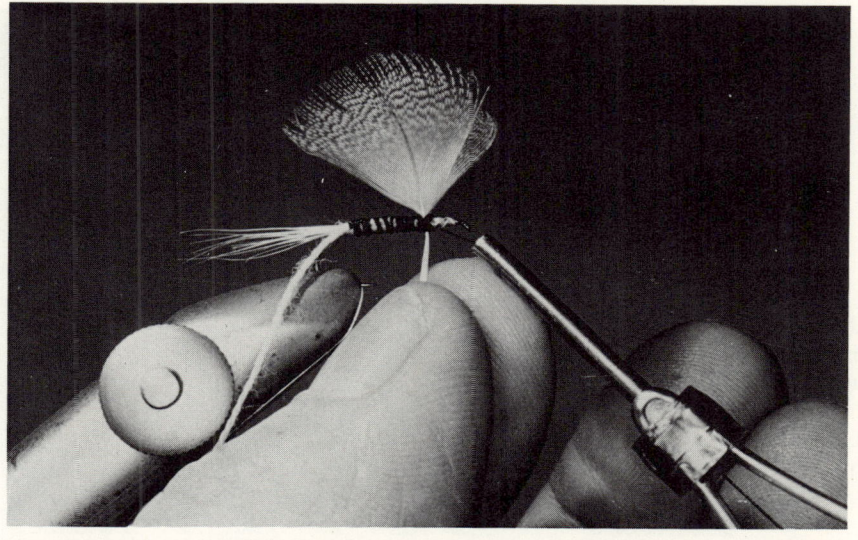

4

Grasp the stems with the left thumb and forefinger under the shank and make four to five turns the other way.

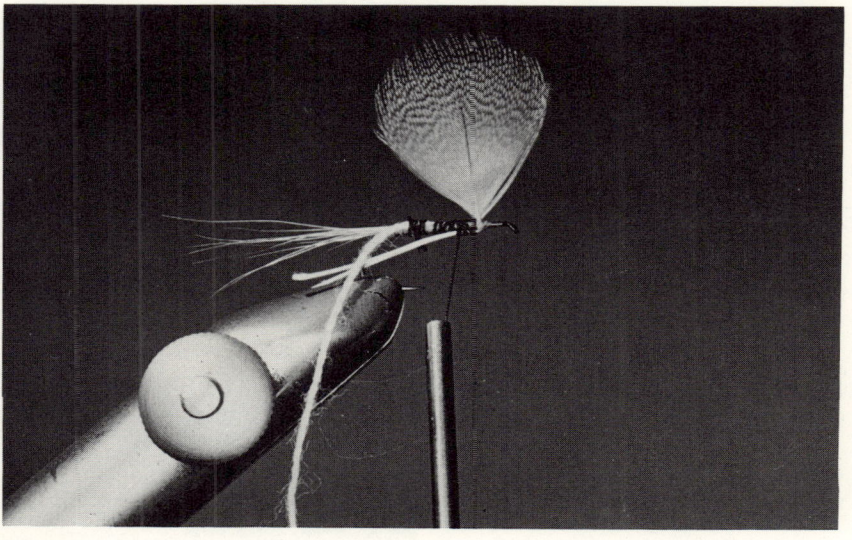

5

Make five or six turns of thread toward the hook bend and fold the stems under along the hook shank. Half-hitch, cut off excess stems, and return the thread to the front of the wing.

6

Wind the body material forward to the wing base, tie off, and half-hitch.

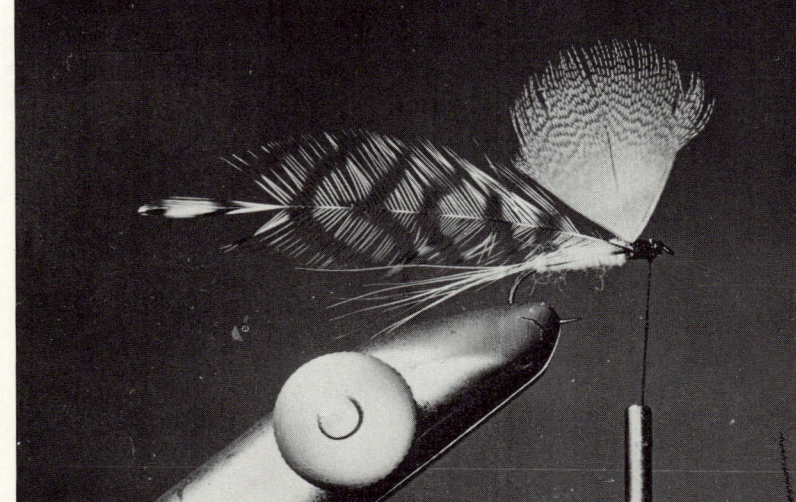

7

Tie in the hackle, shiny (convex) side forward. Note that in preparing the hackle, more fibers have been removed from the upper side of the stem than from the lower. This gives a flat side to wind against the hook shank, causing the fibers to stand out at a 90° angle, and helps prevent rolling of the hackle when winding it on.

8

Make one or two turns of the hackle behind the wing and the balance of turns in front of the wing. Tie off, whip-finish, and add a drop of head cement at the base of the hackle. The fly is complete.

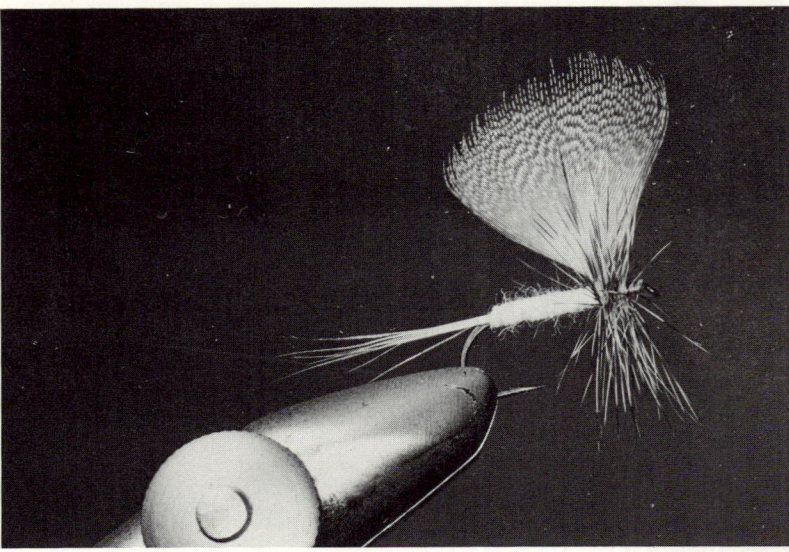

Ted's Crayfish
By THEODORE J. GODFREY
Photographs by James Olmstead

During the last three years this pattern has evolved from a complicated feathered affair to the more practical fly shown here. I had seen some good feather-tied crayfish by Jack Michievicz and had tied some near-enough samples at the request of a friend in southern Pennsylvania. This year I contacted him again and was amazed to hear of his luck with the samples — all six had been lost to good trout! Recently I have fished the hair-tied crayfish and am satisfied that it is at least as good as the old samples. I've seen trout of 2 and 3 pounds move yards to nail this fly. Like the natural, the fly should be fished in short jerks.

I won't say on which streams this fly has been most productive, but I do advise using small, size 8 and 10 ties with very prominent claws — they are necessary, and apparently easily identified by crayfish-hunting trout. The larger sizes of 2 and 4 are great for the bass fisherman, but for trout, the small sizes are preferred. Tie up a few, as they are relaxing work compared to small dry flies, and next time you are on the stream in the cool hush of evening, have a try at catching some of the large trout that hunt crayfish.

MATERIALS
HOOK: Mustad #9671, sizes 2–10
WEIGHT: lead wire
UNDERBODY: light-brown deer hair
OVERBODY: red fox squirrel tail
THORAX: olive chenille
EYES: 50-pound mono
CLAWS: ringneck pheasant body feather
LEGS: ringneck pheasant rump feather
GLUE: Pliobond
THREAD: brown monocord

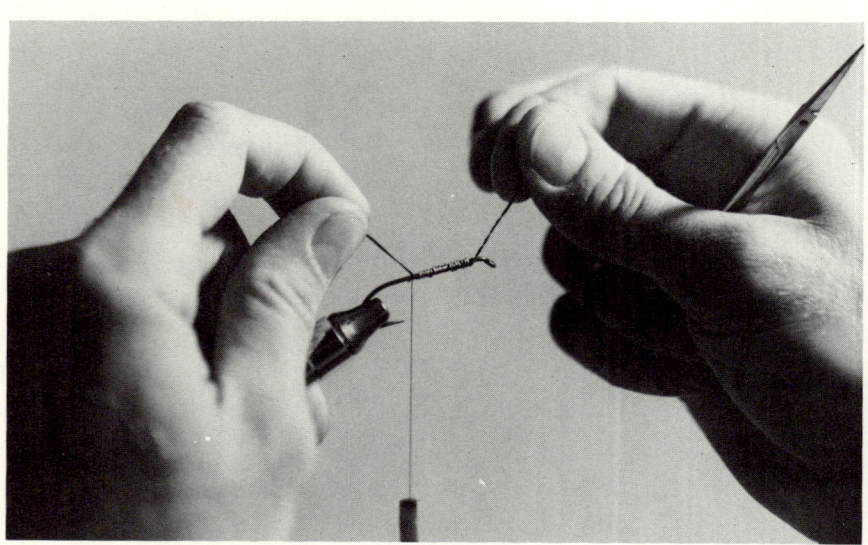

1
On a size 2 hook, wrap tying thread on the hook shank and let it hang approximately two-thirds the length from the eye. Wrap the lead wire over the shank and clip off the loose ends.

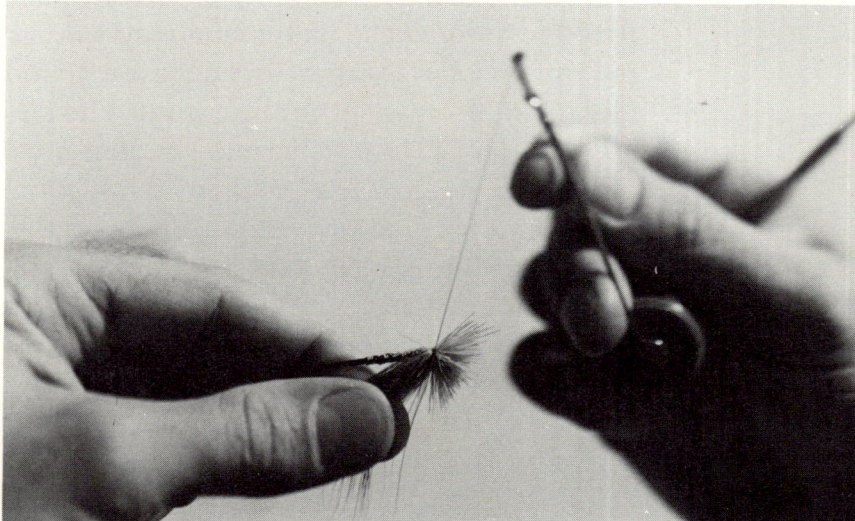

2
Wrap the tying thread to the eye and tie a pencil-sized bunch of light deer hair in under the eye so that the butts extend at least ½ inch beyond the eye. The tips of the hair should extend approximately ½ inch beyond the bend of the hook.

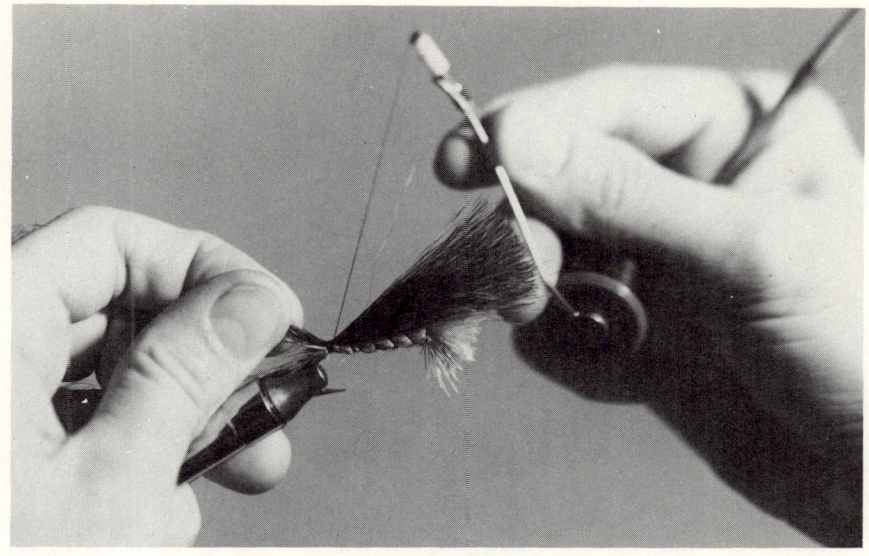

3

Lash the deer hair down on the underside of the hook shank (and lead wrappings) with wide turns of tying thread, and tie tightly with four extra turns at a point on the shank directly above the barb of the hook. Tie red fox squirrel tail hair tightly on top of the shank as shown. The butts of the squirrel hair should be over the eye of the hook and the tips of this hair should be about even with the tips of the deer hair.

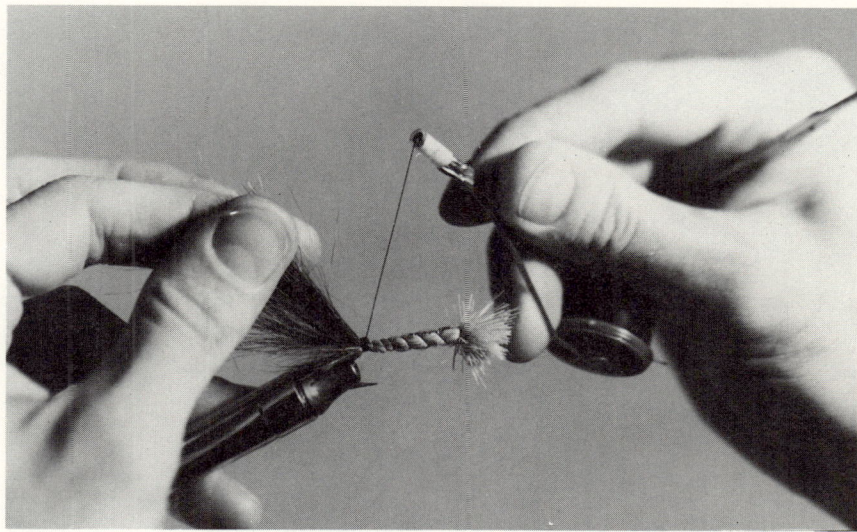

4

Pull the squirrel hair butts back over the bend of the hook and lash down with six tight turns. This produces a small bend or elbow of squirrel hair on top of the shank.

5

In the left hand, the steps in stripping and cutting a claw from a body of feather of a ringneck pheasant. Make two claws and coat them with Pliobond before tying in. Make two eyes by heating the end of heavy monofilament line (right hand). A candle or match will do the job.

6

Looking down on top of the hook shank, lash the eyes down along each side of the body and then put on the claws. The claws should hang down a little since the claw feather stems have some natural curvature. The mono eyes and stems of the claws are lashed down along only *half* of the hook shank.

7

The legs are prepared from a tannish rump feather from the cock ringneck pheasant. Strip off the base fuzz and stroke back the fibers along ½ inch of the stem, exposing the tip fibers.

8

Looking down on top of the hook shank, tie down the tip of the rump feather with the concave side of the feather *up*. The tyings should be up against the squirrel hair elbow.

9

Wrap the tying thread to the center of the hook shank and tie in the stripped end of a piece of olive chenille.

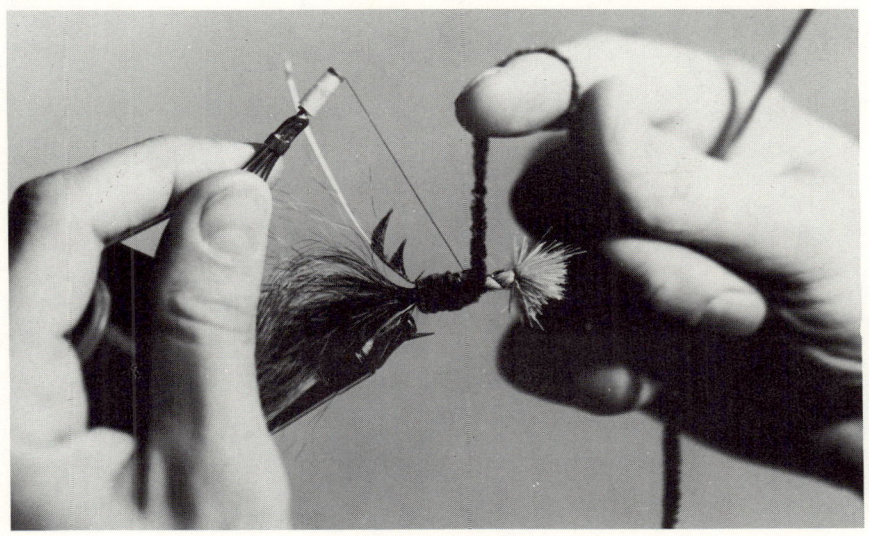

10

Then tightly wrap the chenille over the hook shank up to the eyes and over the wrapped back to the place where it was tied in. Tie down and cut off chenille.

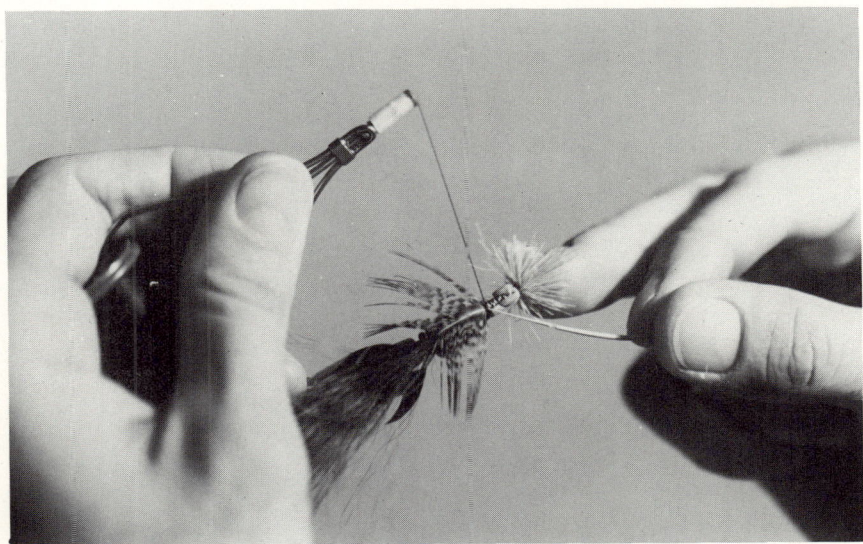

11

Pull the pheasant rump feather down over the back of the chenille and tie it off at the midpoint of the shank. Cut the feather stem off close. The feather fibers should now droop down over the sides of the body.

12
Pull over the back and tie down tightly the squirrel tail hair butts. Don't trim them yet.

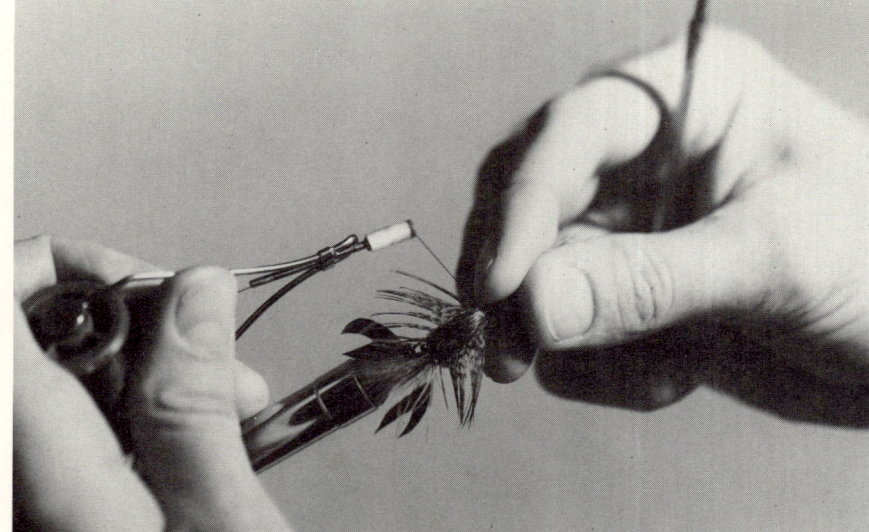

13
Take three wide-spaced wraps of tying thread over the remaining half of the body and tie off close behind the eye.

14
Trim the butts of deer and squirrel hair and coat the tail and back of the crayfish with Pliobond, for a finished fly.

The Matuka Sculpin
By EDWARD GRAHAM
Photographs by James Graham

Successful sculpin fishing requires a fishing method that takes into account the habitat and behavior of the food source to be imitated, and a well-designed fly pattern resulting from a combination of proper tying methods and suitable materials. With these requirements in mind, innovative fly tyers have developed fly-tying techniques that make imitation of the sculpin possible.

Sculpin are found in cold, clear rivers among the rocks and crevices of the stream bed. Imitations must be fished as slowly as possible on, or within inches of, the stream bottom. The angler should use a high-density, sinking fly line and a short leader. Since the sculpin is a poor swimmer, the fly should be allowed to drift naturally, or short sporadic line strips may be used to imitate the erratic darts that characterize the sculpin's movement.

On the Matuka Sculpin, the wing is fastened to the body of the fly by the ribbing. This provides a better silhouette, and prevents the wing from fouling on the hook bend. The sculpin's prominent and easily recognizable physical features — the wide, flat head and the large pectoral fins — must be accurately portrayed if the imitation is to be successful. The sculpin's coloration changes to match the environment, and mottled shades of tan, brown, olive, and black are commonly found. The imitation should be tied to conform with local variations.

MATERIALS
HOOK: Mustad #9672, sizes 1/0–6
WEIGHT: lead wire
TAIL: tan calf hair
BODY: cream sparkle yarn
RIB: narrow gold mylar tinsel
WING: two grizzly hackles dyed brown
PECTORAL FINS: red fox squirrel tail hair
GILLS: red wool dubbing
HEAD: bottom, deer hair dyed light yellow; top, brown deer hair and black deer hair

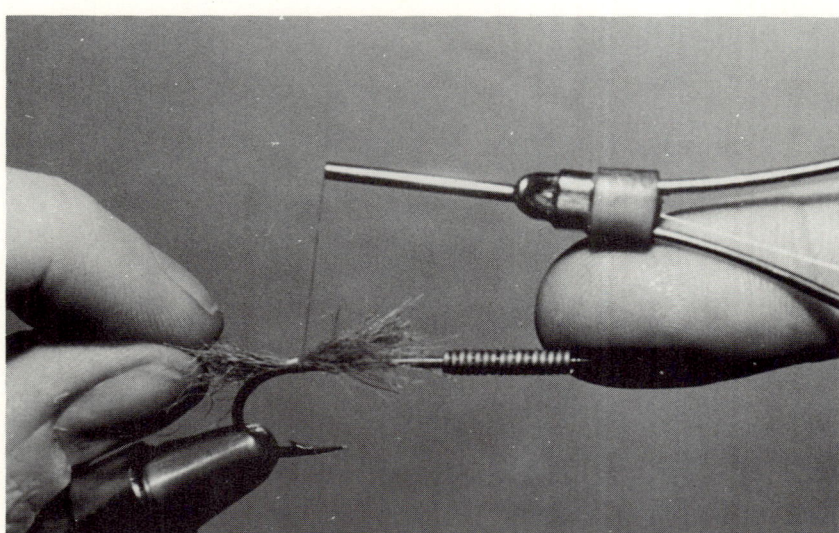

1
Place hook in vise, attach thread, and cover the rear three-quarters of the hook shank with tying thread. Wrap 15 turns of lead wire around the hook shank, ending up at the front of the thread base. Tie in the tan calf tail. Cement the thread and lead wraps.

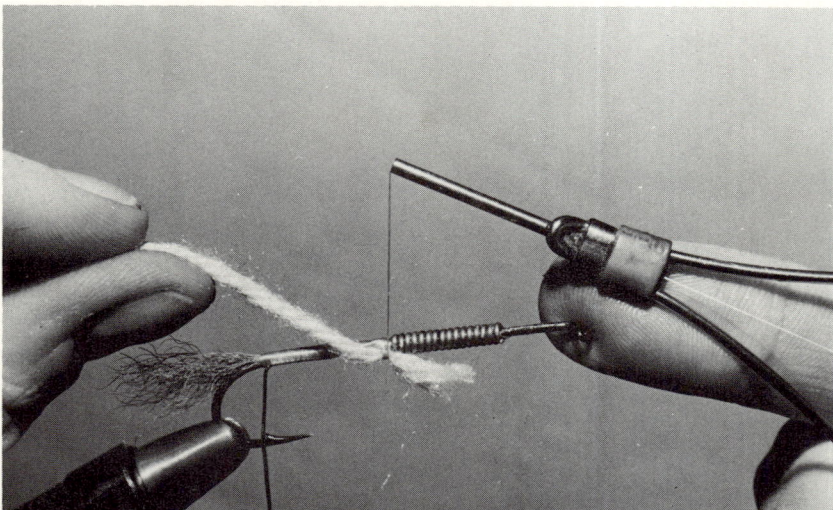

2
Tie in a rib of narrow gold mylar tinsel below the hook shank at the tail position. Advance the thread and tie in 12 inches of cream sparkle yarn behind the lead wire.

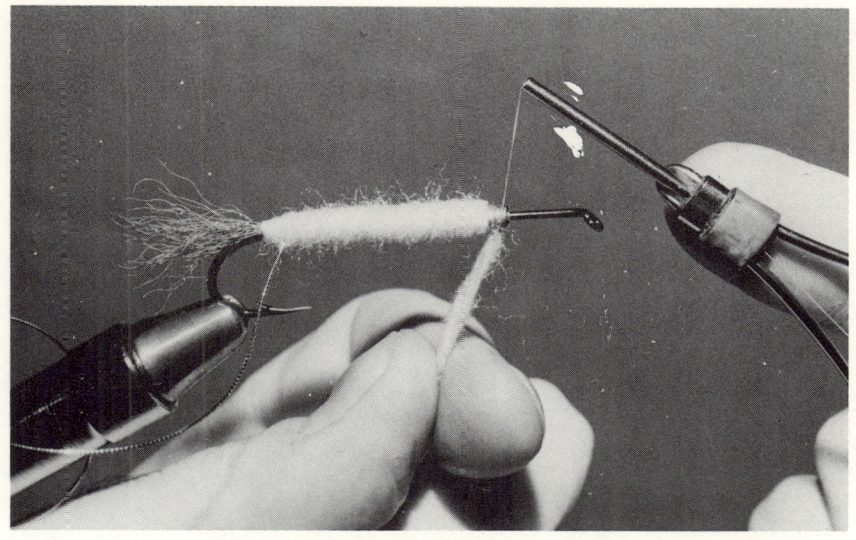

3

Begin the tapered body by wrapping the yarn to the tail. Reverse direction and wind the yarn forward, building a well-proportioned body. Tie yarn off on the final three turns of lead wire. Cement.

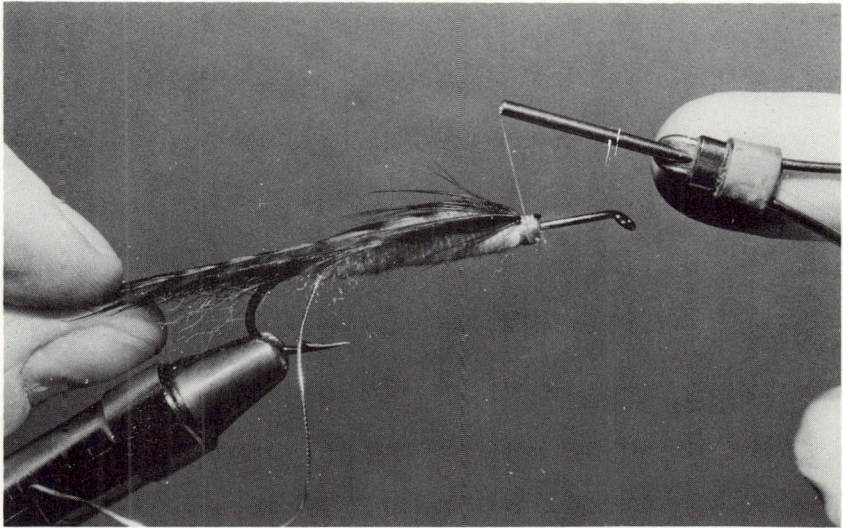

4

Select two matched webby grizzly neck hackles dyed brown. Size them to extend from the lead tie-down area to approximately two-thirds of the hook shank's length past the bend. Place both hackles, one atop the other and with their best sides up, in a horizontal or flat position exactly above the yarn body. Firmly tie in the butt ends of the hackles on top of the lead tie-down area. Cement.

5

To prepare the feathers for the Matuka wing, grasp the hackle tips with the left hand. Maintaining the horizontal position of the hackles, use the right thumb and forefinger to stroke forward all hackle fibers from the bend to the tie-down area. Use the right hand to spiral the gold tinsel up the body between the spread hackle fibers, lashing the hackle stems firmly to the top of the body. Tie the tinsel off in the same manner as the yarn body. Use the bodkin to free any hackle fibers tied down in the ribbing process. Cement.

6

To imitate the pectoral fins, tie a small bunch of red fox squirrel tail hair on the near side of the hook in the tie-down area. The waste ends of the hair must not extend into the first quarter of the hook shank, so the butt ends should be cut flush with the leading edge of the tie-down area. Tie in a similar bunch of squirrel tail hair on the far side of the hook. Cement.

7

To imitate the gills and to conceal the tie-down area, spin a red wool dubbing onto the thread. Wrap forward, completely covering all the thread windings. Then advance the thread to the bare shank.

8

Prepare a bunch of dun-brown deer hair dyed light yellow, and position it atop the hook behind the gills by taking two or three loose turns of thread around the hair clump. The tips should point toward the bend and should not extend past the squirrel hair.

9

Begin increasing the pressure on the hair by slowly tightening the turns of thread encircling it. As the pressure increases, the hair will begin to flare. Allow the hair to roll under the hook, and hold it there with finger pressure. Wrap two tight turns of thread to lock the hair in place on the hook bottom.

10

Prepare a bunch of deer hair dyed brown and position it on top of the hook with two turns of thread. Increase the thread pressure on the hair while holding it with the left hand, and flare it in place. Take a smaller clump of black deer hair and flare it directly on top of the brown hair. This process will form a deer-hair head that is light in color on the bottom and mottled dark on top. Be sure to keep each separate color of hair in its proper place.

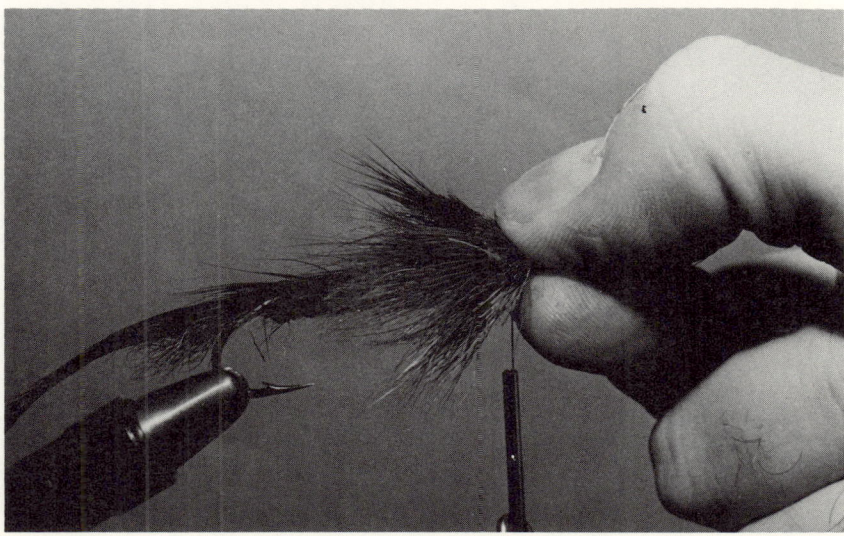

11

Advance the thread to the hook shank in front of the hair. Using the fingers of the right hand, push the hair firmly to the rear, jamming it hard against the tie-down area. Secure with several turns of thread taken up against the base of the hair.

12

Begin again with the light-yellow hair, and flare and position it on the bottom of the hook. Flare the brown deer hair, followed by the black, atop the hook shank. Advance the thread to the front of the hair. Use the right hand to firmly push the hair back against the body, clearing the eye of the hook. Complete with a whip finish.

13

Keeping the scissors points nearly parallel to the shank, trim the deer hair on the bottom to a flat shape, allowing the red wool gills to show through the remaining light-yellow deer hair tips.

14

Trim the top and sides of the deer hair to a broad, oval-shaped head. Be careful not to cut the hair tips, but allow them to extend backwards to help simulate fins.

15

Apply head cement to the whip finish. If desired, a coat of thin rod varnish may be applied to the underside of the head to help maintain its shape. The fly is now finished.

The Pre-Emerger Nymph
By HAL W. JANSSEN
Photographs by Bill Rhodes

A considerable amount of my fishing has been visual, which has offered me an opportunity to observe not only the fish but also the mannerisms and characteristics of the varied range of aquatic insects. The baetis nymph is the most predominant of all mayflies in our ponds and lakes in the western part of the United States. Ten years ago, I developed the Pre-Emerger Nymph for cruising trout in lakes and ponds. When tied in different-length hooks, different sizes, and different colors, it will match any still-water mayfly nymph available.

The weighting of the nymph is essential, as its best presentation is while the fly is dropping and the lead affords a smooth and quiet entry through the surface. By altering the size of the lead and hook and the amount of turns, different rates of sink can be achieved, as well as varied depths. The use of the weighted body also allows for quick entry when you are casting directly to a cruising fish.

Down through the years, I have found that all tail materials become brittle after use and susceptible to damage from the fishes' teeth. The use of dyed golden pheasant tippet as tail material eliminated this problem, totally, as well as imitating the fringed tails found on all baetis nymphs. By choosing the dark or light shades of golden pheasant tippets, different shades can be attained with the same color of dye. I chose rabbit for the body because of its water-absorbent qualities and its availability as a fly-tying material. The ease with which rabbit takes to dye and its range of natural colors, such as white and grey, make it the perfect body material for nymphs.

The mottled-turkey wing case looks most realistic when epoxied. The epoxy can also be considered a form of weight to help draw the nymph down, as well as adding durability to fragile areas. Here color is important: a white-tipped turkey, or anything that is darkly mottled black and brown, would be a fair substitute. Adding the additional bulge of fur just at the base of the wing case allows for smooth positioning when it is pulled over, leaving absolutely no shallow or low spot in the thorax.

The nymph offers two choices of leg styles: one with a splayed look and one with the traditional positioning on the bottom side of the body. Through observation, I have found that the natural nymph goes through a period of pre-emergence before hatching, similar to a runner's warming up by jogging before a race. This pre-emergence is a series of lifts from the weed beds of several inches to a foot, then a slow sink or draw back. While the nymph is returning to the weed beds, it curls its body slightly up and extends its legs and tail in a splayed manner, as if anticipating touching the top of the weed. The splayed leg position imitates this phase perfectly. The standard style of leg can be used for imitating migrating nymphs, where the leg position is not so important.

Although the nymph was originally developed for lakes and ponds, over the past several years it has become widely accepted for slow-moving streams and spring creeks. It has accounted for rainbows up to 15 pounds, brown trout of 13 pounds, and steelhead up to 20 pounds in California. The natural shape, ease of tying, and durability of the Pre-emerger Nymph should lend itself to other uses on streams and lakes throughout the country.

MATERIALS

HOOK: Mustad #9672, size 16
TAIL: golden pheasant tippet, dyed medium olive
BODY: grey rabbit fur, dyed medium olive; olive thread rib
WING CASE: mottled turkey feather, brown in color
LEGS: prime natural wood-duck flank-feather fibers

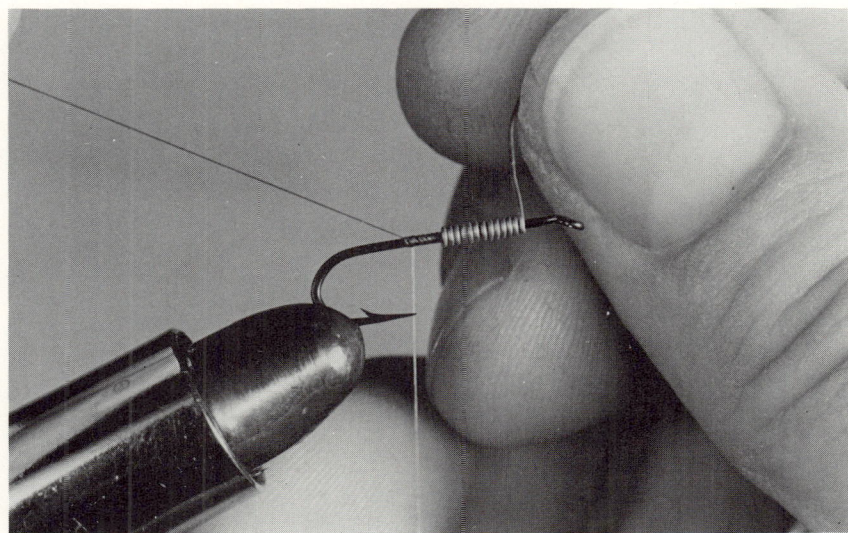

1

Start the thread on the hook ⅛ inch to the rear of the eye and wind to a position directly above the hook point. Do not cut excess thread at the start of the wrapping of the thread back on itself as this will eventually be used as the body rib; instead, attach the excess thread to a thread holder to keep it out of the way. Wind 1 amp lead over the thread 13 turns toward the eye of the hook to the start of the thread wraps.

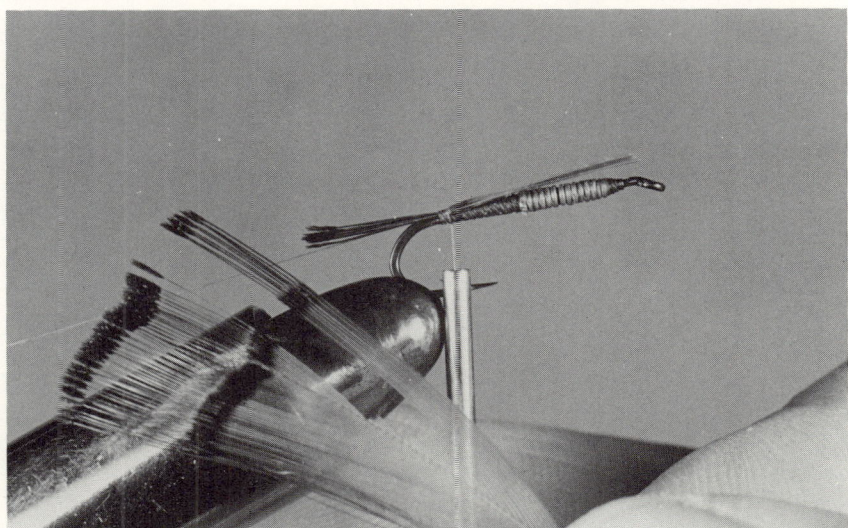

2

Cap the lead front and back with the thread, then taper the body base from front to rear. A smooth, even base is essential for a smooth, even body. Cut seven or eight fibers for the tail from a golden pheasant tippet that has been dyed medium olive, and secure in a tight bunch on top of the hook. The tail length should be no longer than the gap of the hook. Cut the golden pheasant tippet butt even with the start of the lead; this will be used as a pad, and adds additional strength to the tail fibers. The body rib will still protrude to the rear of the hook in thread holder.

3

Grey rabbit fur, dyed medium olive, is dubbed directly to the prewaxed olive thread. Spin the fur to tighten, and wind clockwise toward the eye of the hook. It should now be in a position three-fourths of the way up the hook shank. The body taper is formed not by the amount of fur but by the shape of the thread and lead base.

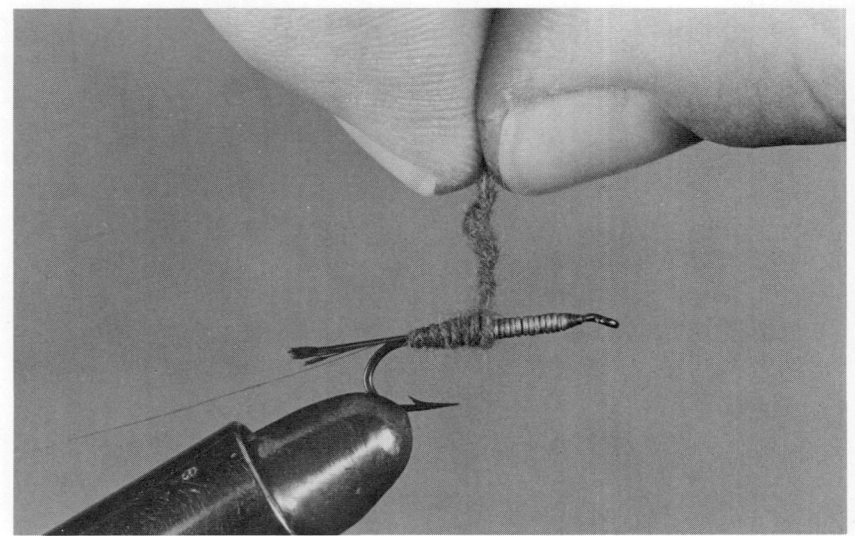

4

Remove the thread rib from the holder and take one turn over the base of the tail, then one turn applied directly under the tail, and pull tight. This will splay the tightly bunched fibers and fan them at right angles to the left and right of the rear of the hook shank. From this point, take the thread in even segments, allowing for a slight amount of cutting into the fur, and wind to the position of the thread and bobbin.

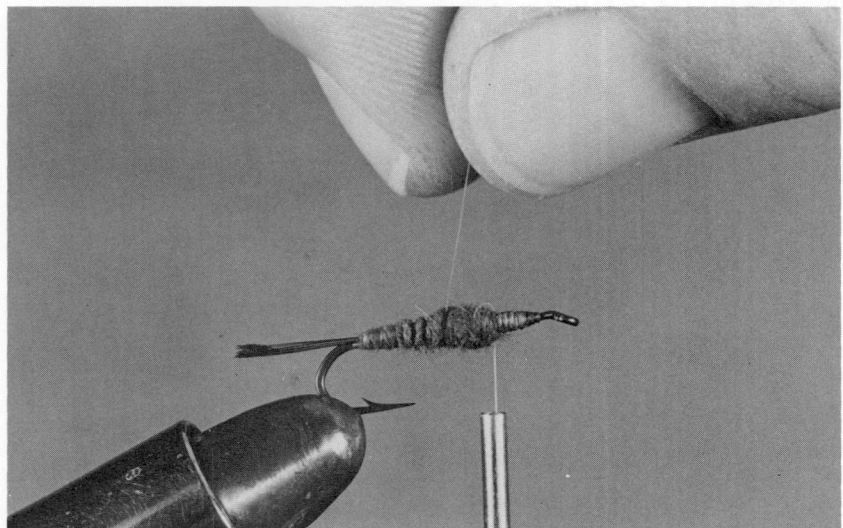

5

After the thread is wound over, secure the dubbing and wind over some of the body dubbing to a halfway point on the hook. Cut a darkly mottled turkey feather, brown in color, at the base, approximately half again as wide as the fur body, or approximately 10 fibers in width. Tie it in directly on top by starting a little to the tyer's side of the hook, which will allow the turkey to rotate directly to the top of the hook position and evenly to each side.

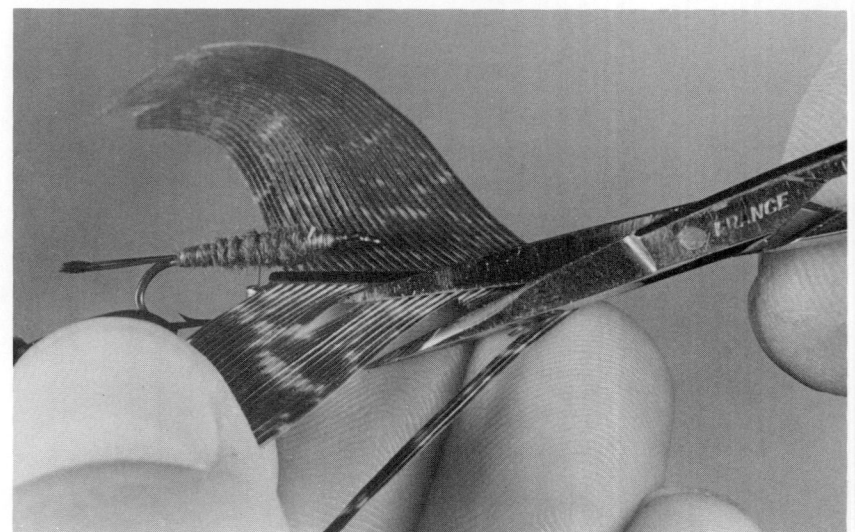

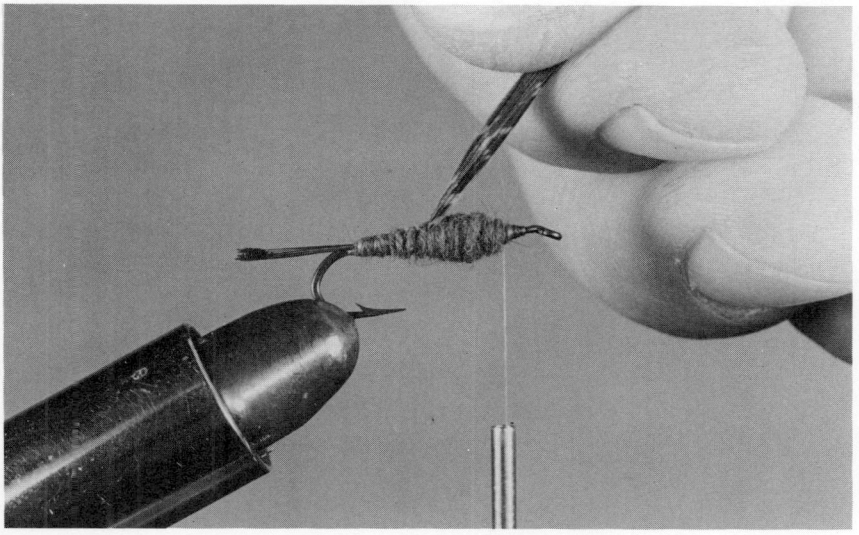

6

After the turkey feather is tied in for the wing case, rabbit fur, dyed medium olive, is used again for the thorax, with two additional turns of fur applied at the base of the wing case. Wind the fur to the front of the hook, allowing ⅛ inch in front of the eye for head and legs. Pull the wing case forward and secure.

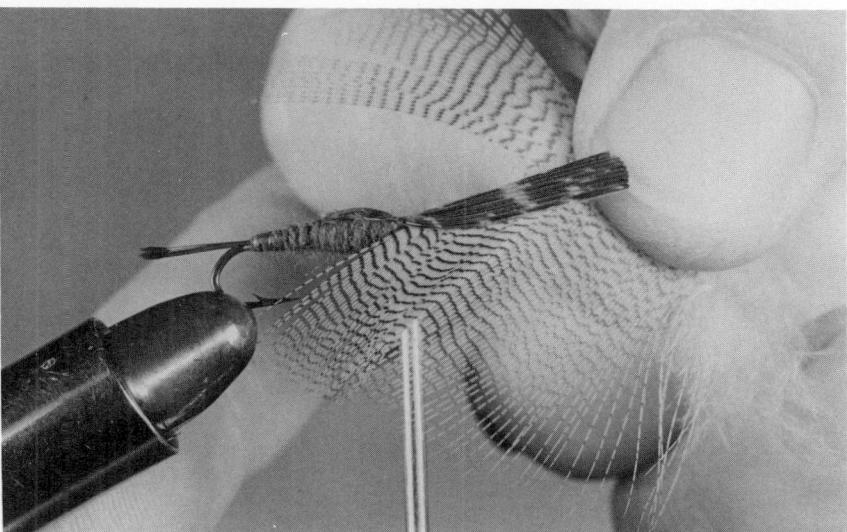

7

To make the legs, select a prime, natural, wood-duck flank feather. The curve on the left side of the feather fibers will be applied to the left, or tyer's, side of the hook, and the fibers from the right side of the quill will be applied to the right side of the hook to obtain the proper leg curvature.

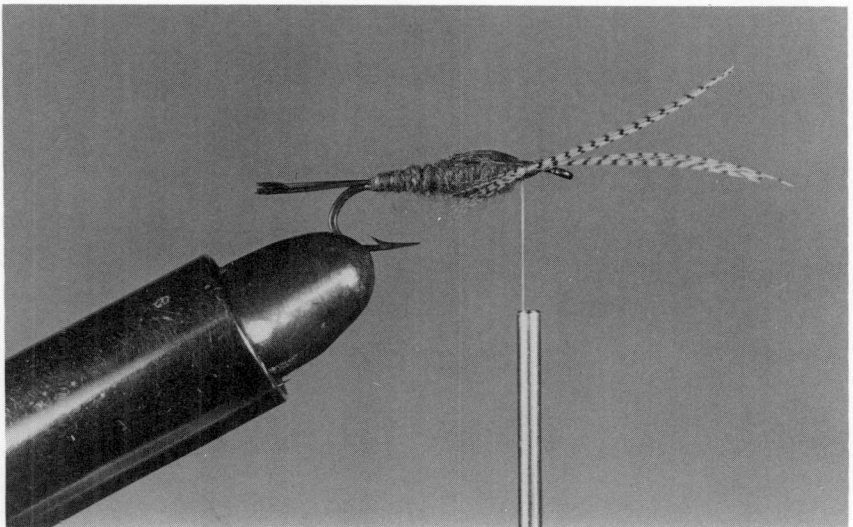

8

Tie the wood-duck feathers into place and position the stems properly. Plenty of room should have been left to attach the legs and to finish off the head.

9

Pull the legs up to the proper length with approximately six to seven wraps to hold them securely. When pulling on the fibers, always hold the hook with the finger as the upward pressure is applied to obtain the proper leg length. This will prevent opening of the gape of the hook, as well as allowing for the proper amount of pressure to be applied to the stems of the wood duck, not allowing it to be pulled clear out from underneath the thread, which so often happens.

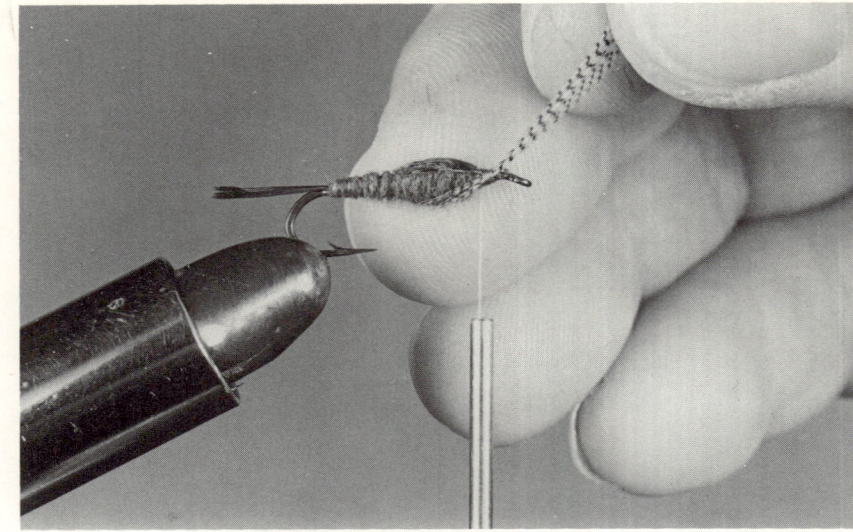

10

Using the figure-8 method with the thread, splay the legs at right angles to the hook: Take the thread over the top and behind the legs on the side of the hook and apply pressure toward the eye of the hook. Make two turns around the head, then take the thread behind the legs on the tyer's side, again applying pressure toward the eye. Then make two to three turns around the head of the fly.

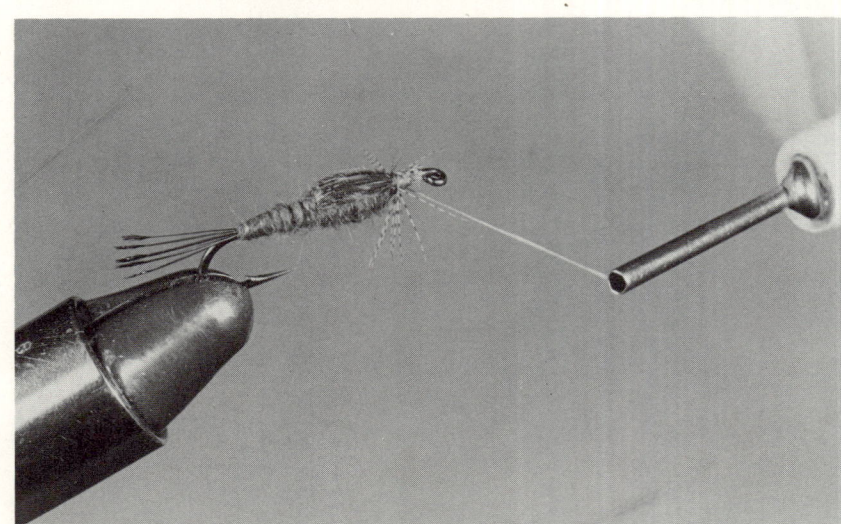

11

Carefully epoxy the wing case. This adds durability and weight, as well as imitating the shiny, glassy look that the natural mayfly nymph attains just before emerging. Using a slow-drying epoxy will leave the materials flexible, whereas the hard, brittle effect achieved with the quick-drying types will turn white and crack with any amount of use. Note the amount of splaying in the tail and legs, the effect of the fringe on the tail from the use of pheasant tippets, and the speckled, lifelike effect of the legs near the front of the finished fly.

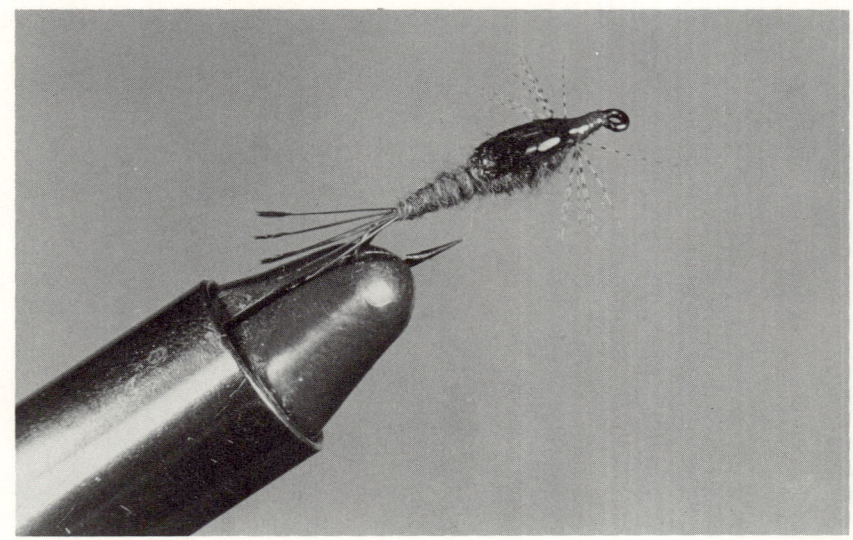

The Cotton-Thread Stonefly Nymph
By CHARLES KROM
Photographs by Ron Kusse

To most fly tyers, experimenting with new ideas for patterns can be a challenging pasttime. A carefully thought-up idea that is worked into a productive trout fly is but one of the gratifying rewards of time spent at the vise. It was one of those tying sessions that brought me to solving a problem of duplicating peacock quill. I had always liked stripped peacock quills for bodies on my stonefly nymphs, but it limited me to small patterns. The need for large sizes to match the waters I fished led me to experiment. I wanted a body that looked like stripped quill and was long enough to tie up to sizes 6 and 8. Thus I struck on the idea of marrying one strand each of light- and dark-brown cotton thread to two strands of off-white. The result was a close copy of Mother Nature that became a deadly pattern.

By using the large selection of commercially dyed colors and shades of thread and a selected amount of strands, different patterns and sizes can be worked out. Applying several coats of lacquer and a final coat of satin finish varnish will make a durable nymph.

Incidentally, the use of cotton thread is not limited to nymphs. It can help make excellent dry-fly imitations, and the color combinations are as broad as the tyer's imagination and skill.

MATERIALS

HOOK: #9672 3X Mustad Model Perfect, sizes 6–12
TAILS: two peccary fibers
BODY: white floss underbody; cotton thread, one dark brown, one light brown, and two off-white
THORAX: creamy fox fur
WING CASE: feathers from the shoulder of a peacock wing
LEGS: brown hackle

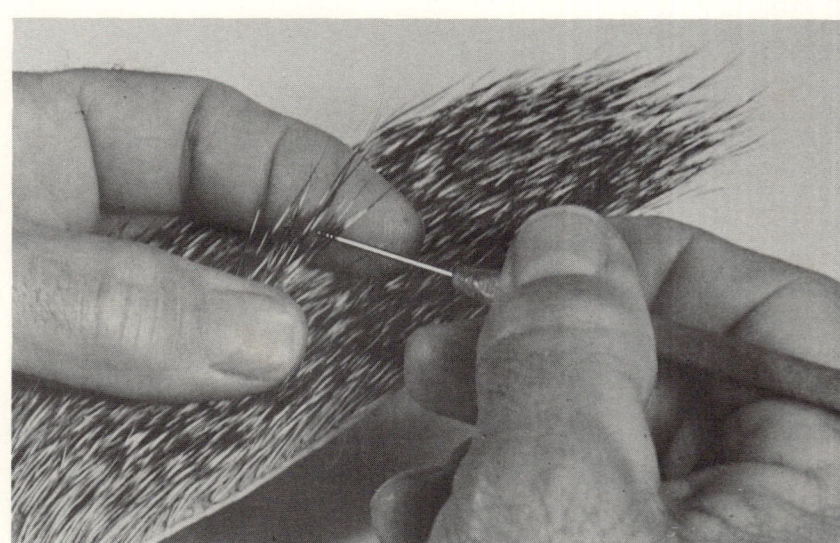

1

Select two matching fibers from a piece of peccary hide. Make sure the fiber tips have enough brown so that no white will show when the tails are tied on the hook.

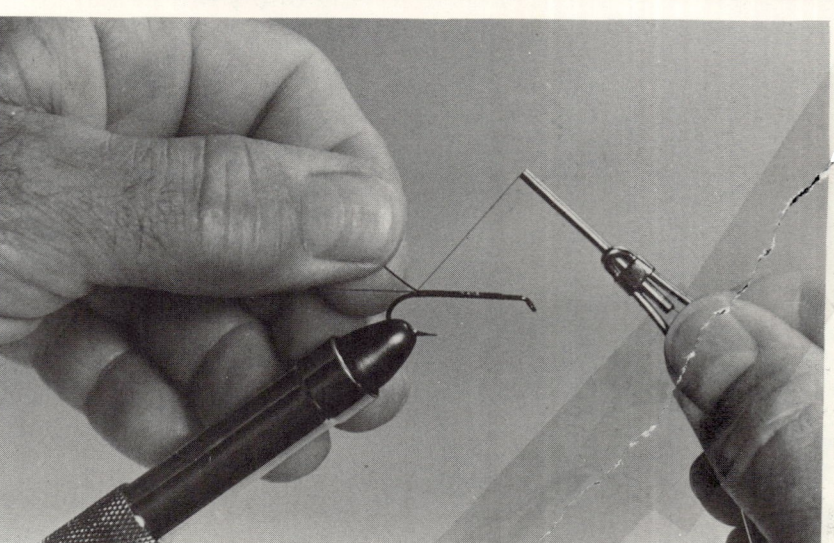

2

Clamp a size 8 hook in a vise and wrap the shank with tying thread. Holding the two peccary fibers together, measure the tail length and tie them down on the hook shank. When the fibers are secure, divide the tails with thread, forming a slight fork. The tail length is determined by measuring the fibers to half the length of the hook.

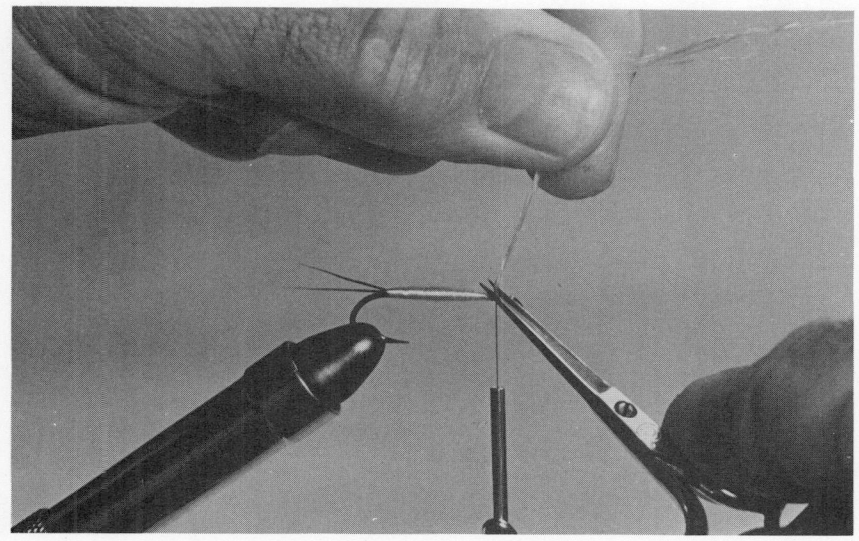

3

Select a length of white nylon floss and tie one end to the middle of the hook shank. Carefully work the floss back and forth on the hook, forming an even, cigar-shaped underbody ending at the eye.

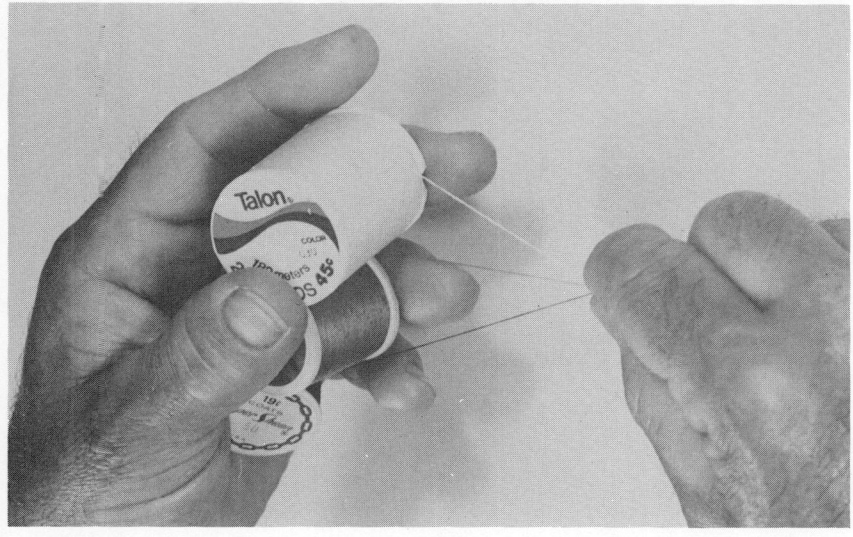

4

Select one strand each of light- and dark-brown cotton thread to two strands of off-white.

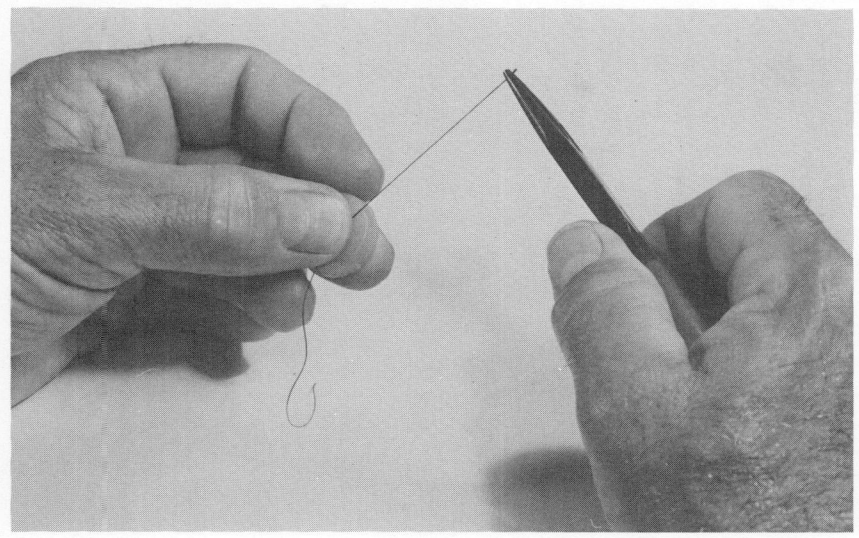

5

Lightly wax each strand. This will aid in keeping married strands together.

6

Marry one dark-brown to one light-brown strand, then to the two off-white strands. The colors must be married in this order to match that of a stripped peacock quill. Tie in all four strands to the underside of the floss underbody, the full length of the body, to assure an even taper during the next step.

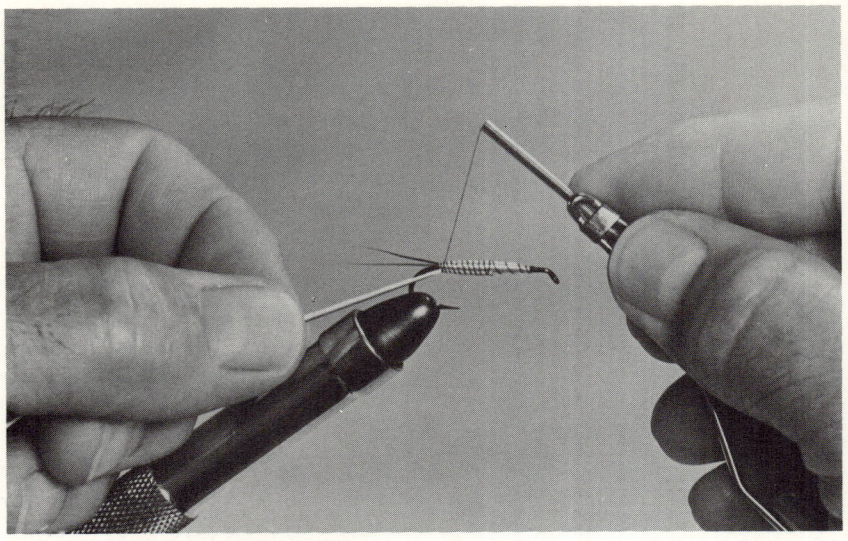

7

Carefully wind the married strands up the tapered underbody, checking to see if all four strands are adhering to each other as you wind. When enough winds have been made for the desired body length, tie down the threads and cut off any excess.

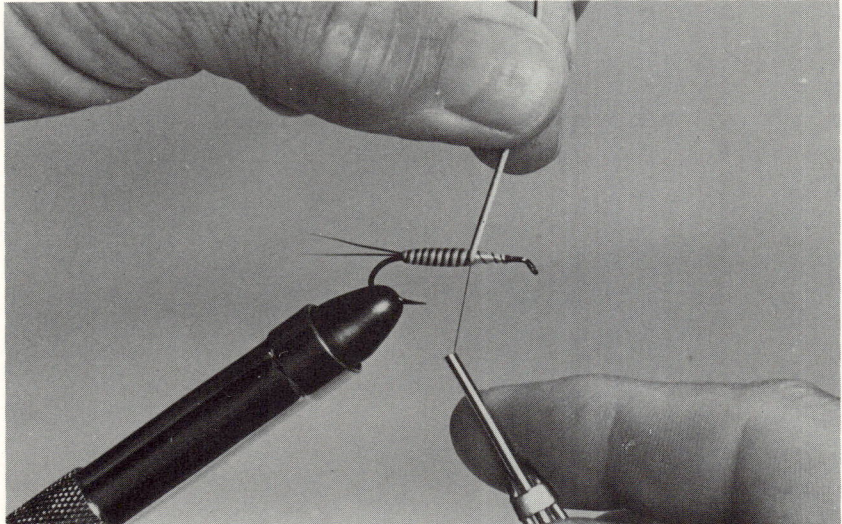

8

Apply at least four coats of a good grade of lacquer to attain smoothness, then apply a final coat of satin varnish to tone down the body. Allow enough time for the varnish to dry before proceeding to the next step. Dubbing too soon might absorb the varnish and change the color.

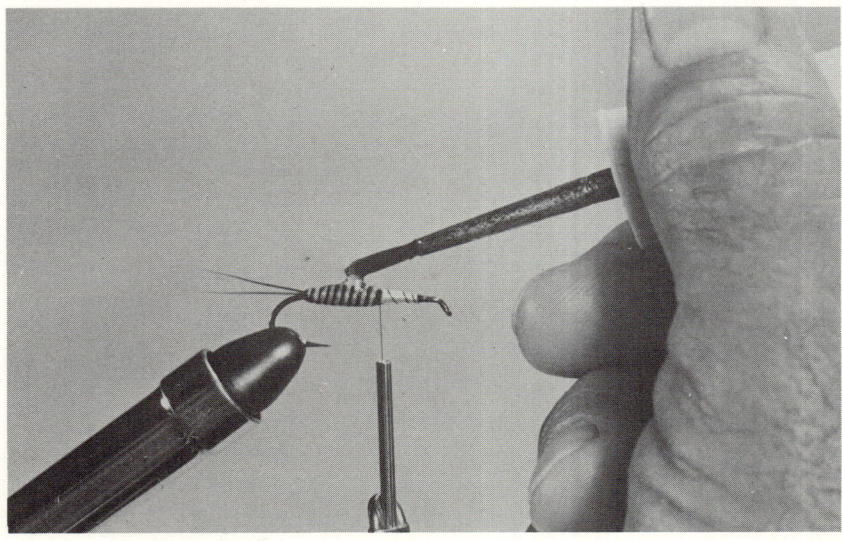

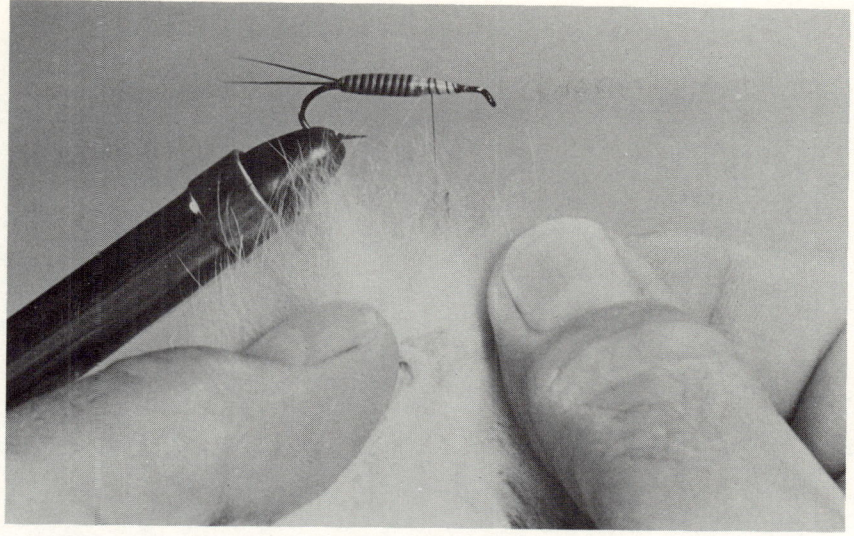

9

For the thorax, select a creamy fox fur for dubbing. For photography reasons, black tying thread was used here, but white thread is preferable because it does not show through the cotton thread wrapping or the fur dubbing.

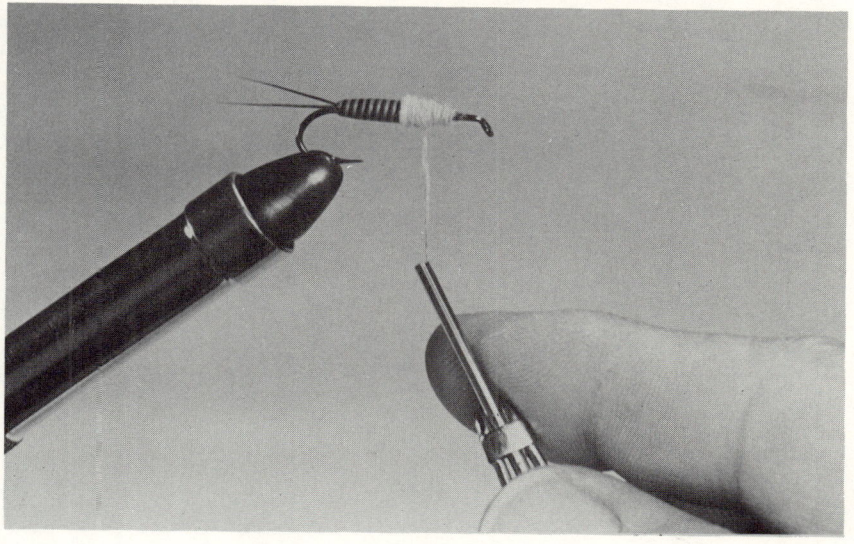

10

After dubbing fox fur to the waxed thread, measure the thorax by wrapping half the entire body with the fur dubbing.

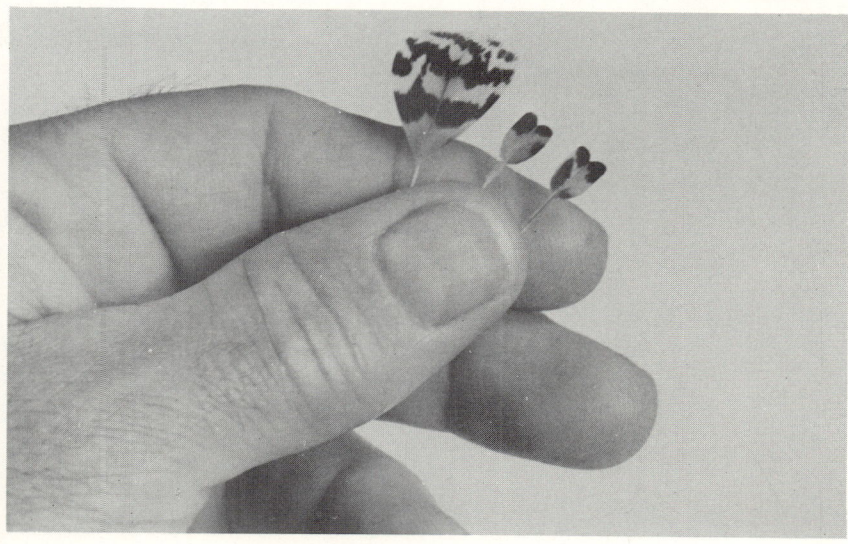

11

Select two feathers from a peacock wing shoulder and coat with a clear plastic spray. After it is set, cut to desired size and shape. For hook sizes 8 and larger, you will need two wing cases; smaller sizes require only one feather.

12

Select a semi-dry brown hackle and stroke the barbules perpendicular to the quill. With a sharp razor or X-Acto knife, cut the hackle into three sections. Glue the sections together with a waterproof adhesive. When it is dry, trim the hackle to fit the length of the wing case.

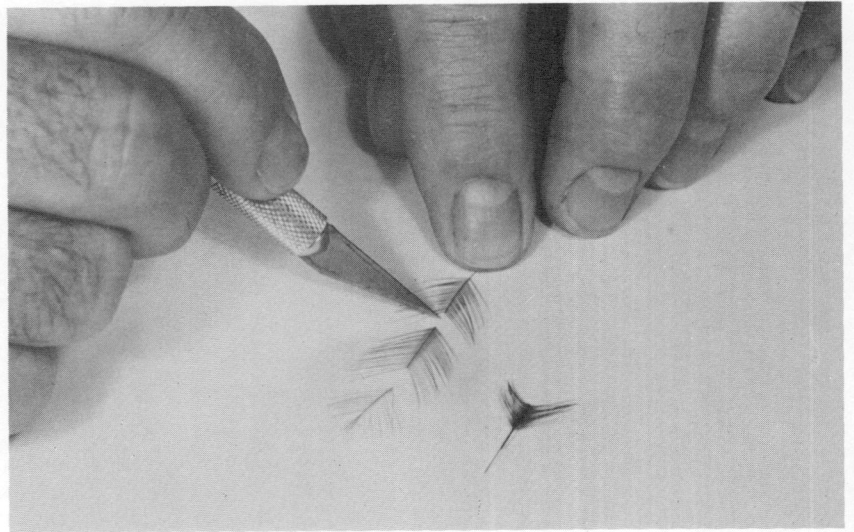

13

After the two wing cases have been glued together, add a drop of adhesive to the top of the hackle legs and glue to the underside of the wing case. The final gluing is done by applying two coats of adhesive to the underside of the wing case and leg assembly and the top part of the thorax.

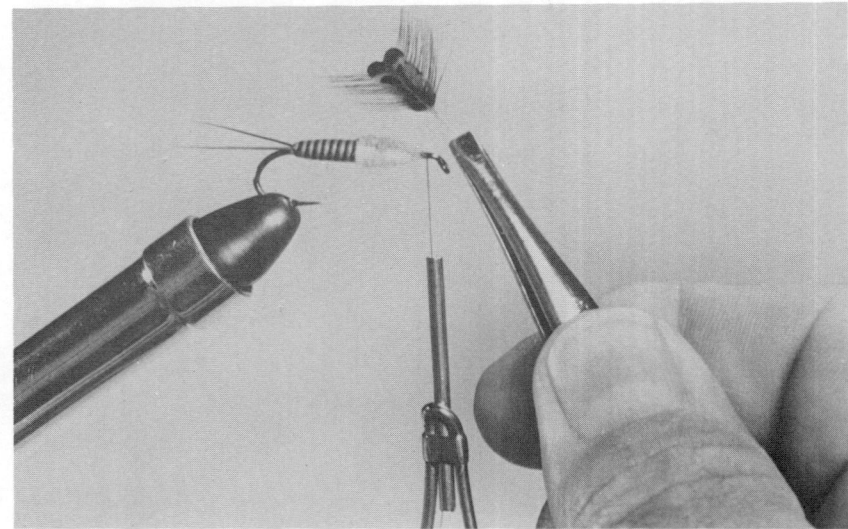

14

With the adhesive tacky, gently lay the wing case and leg assembly on top of the thorax and check for correct positioning. If the wing case assembly lines up properly on the thorax, gently press down with the index finger until both adhere. This is a crucial step requiring care and judgment.

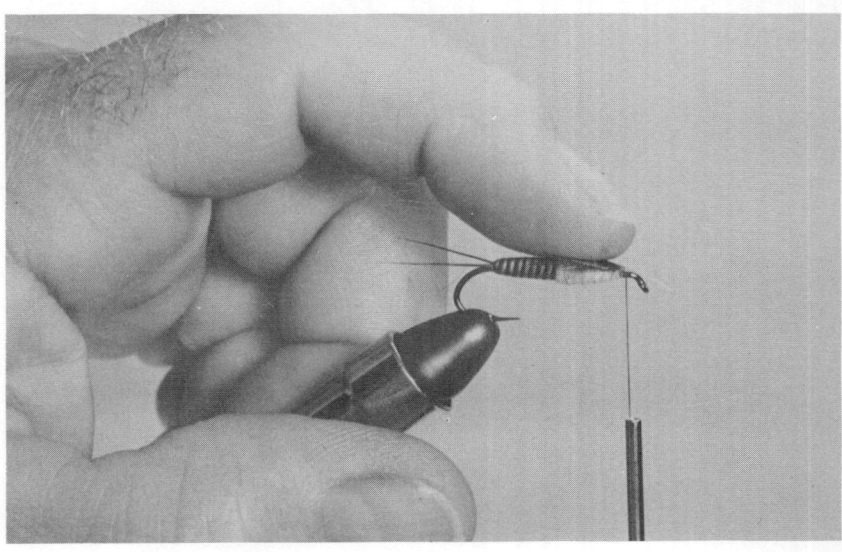

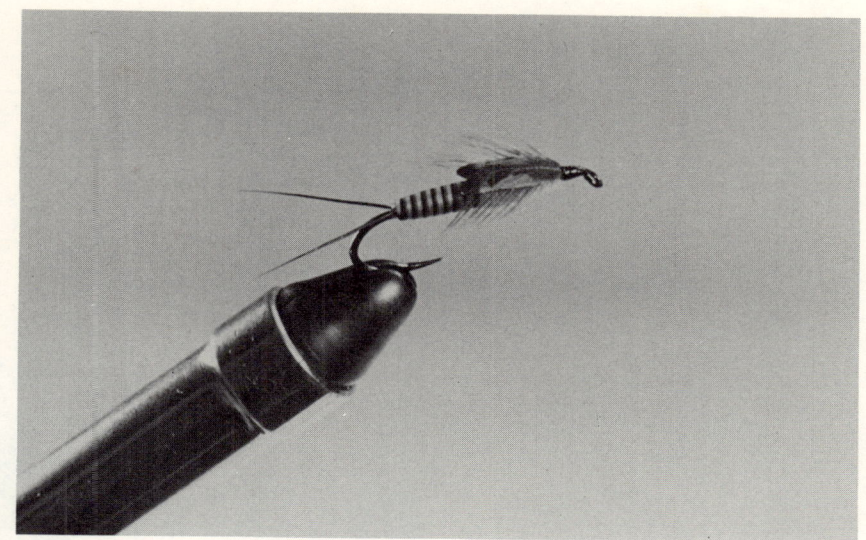

15
Bind down the hackle stems and cut off the excess. Complete the fly with a whip finish and lacquer the head. Finally, carefully coat the wing case and head with satin varnish, and the fly is complete.

The Emergent Caddis Pupa
By GARY LAFONTAINE
Photographs by Glenn Zander

Bill Saunders once scolded me in his newspaper column: "[LaFontaine] says that random fishing is no way to test a new fly, but I've used his Sparkling Caddis Pupa randomly all season now and I, for one, am convinced that these fantastically effective patterns will revolutionize fly fishing theories on the caddis."

Of course, I'm not against the successes of "random" fishing. Such experiences are the trial-and-error testing that any fly must go through before it becomes accepted by fly fishermen, but before the Sparkling Caddis imitations were ever written about or sold commercially they were tested in a different way.

The radical concepts of these patterns — the use of a translucent material (trilobal nylon) that reflects light to imitate the air bubble carried by the natural pupa, the omission of wing pads, and the need for both deep and emergent imitations — were tested by scuba-diving observation. It was underwater, actually watching selective trout accept or reject simulations of the naturals, where it was decided that the Sparkling Caddis Pupa looked correct to the fish.

Each caddis genus has both deep and emergent imitations because a different stages of the hatch, trout feed at different levels. The Deep Pupa is fished dead drift, designed to bounce the bottom currents. The Emergent Pupa is fished semi-dry in the film, either drag-free or with upstream twitches.

MATERIALS
HOOK: Mustad Viking #94840, sizes 16–20
OVERBODY: grey Sparkle yarn
UNDERBODY: grey fur
WING: grey speckled (Coastal) deer hair
HEAD: grey marabou strands

1
Prepare the Sparkle yarn — which is available by the skein from most fabric shops or by the card from many fly fishing shops — by separating the individual plies of the four-ply yarn.

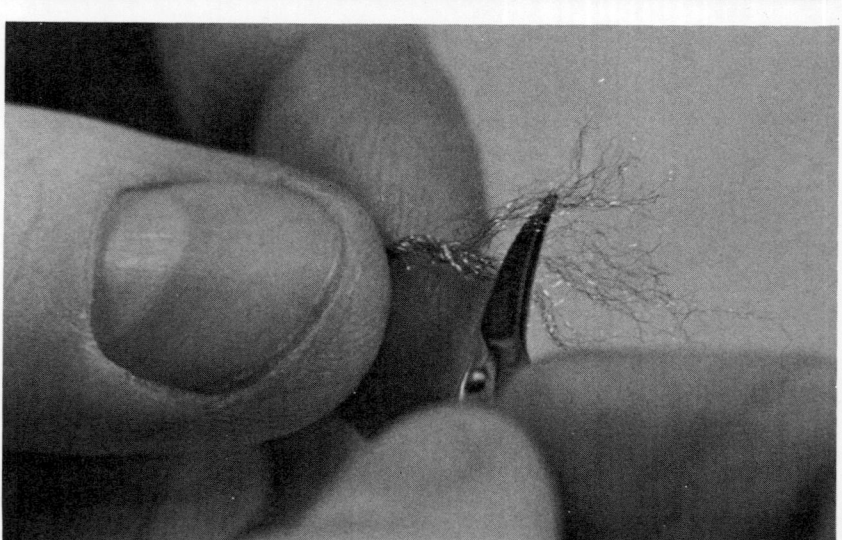

2
This material is the key for simulating the transparent, air-filled sheath of the emerging pupa. Fray one of the plies with a scissors point or bodkin until the filaments are separated completely.

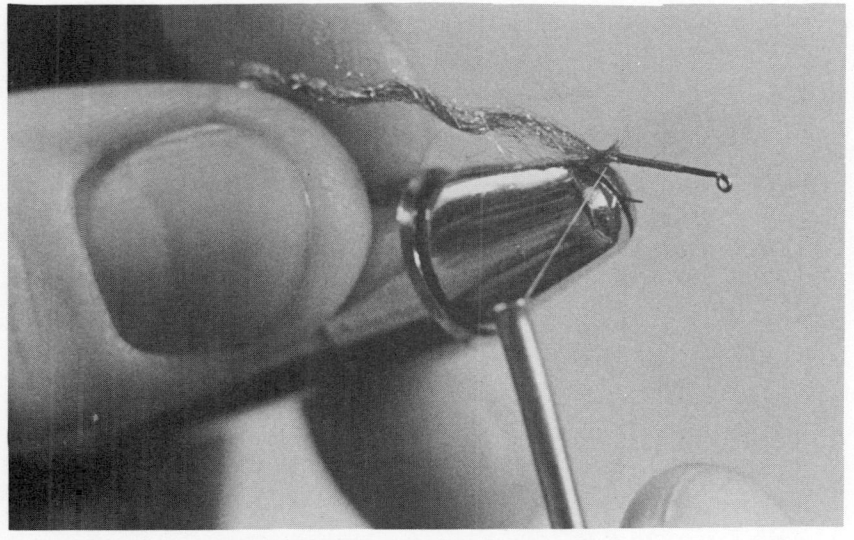

3
Start forming the overbody by tying the frayed ply to the top of the shank at the bend of the hook.

4
Repeat steps 1 through 3, but this time tie the frayed ply to the bottom of the hook shank. Leave both of these strands, top and bottom, dangling temporarily.

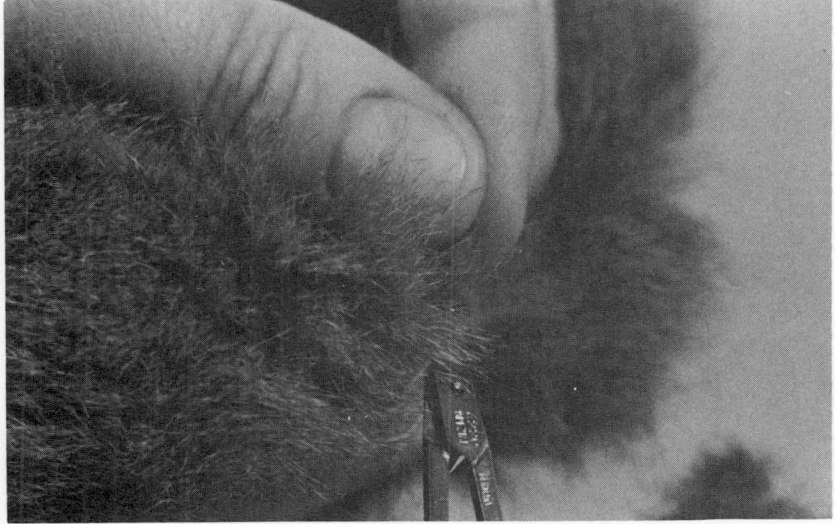

5
For the underbody, clip grey rabbit fur from the skin into a fine dubbing. (Chopped polypropolene can be used as a substitute.)

6

Spin the fur onto the thread. To form a thin body, pinch sparse clumps of fur from the dubbing wad and work along the thread with the thumb and forefinger. Apply this dubbing evenly.

7

Wrap the fur-covered thread neatly on the hook shank approximately three-fourths of the way toward the eye.

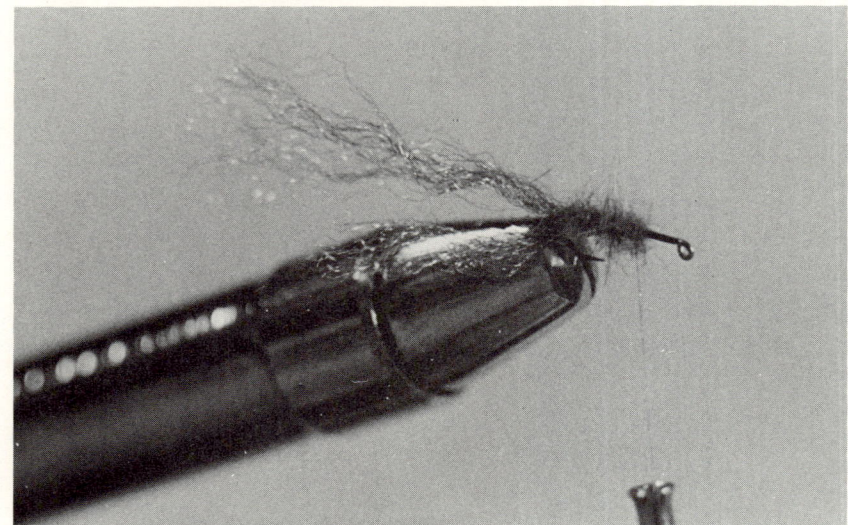

8

Draw the top of the overbody, previously left dangling, loosely forward and tie it down in front of the underbody. Spread these filaments so that they envelop the top half of the underbody.

9
Draw the bottom of the overbody loosely forward and spread it to envelop the bottom half of the underbody.

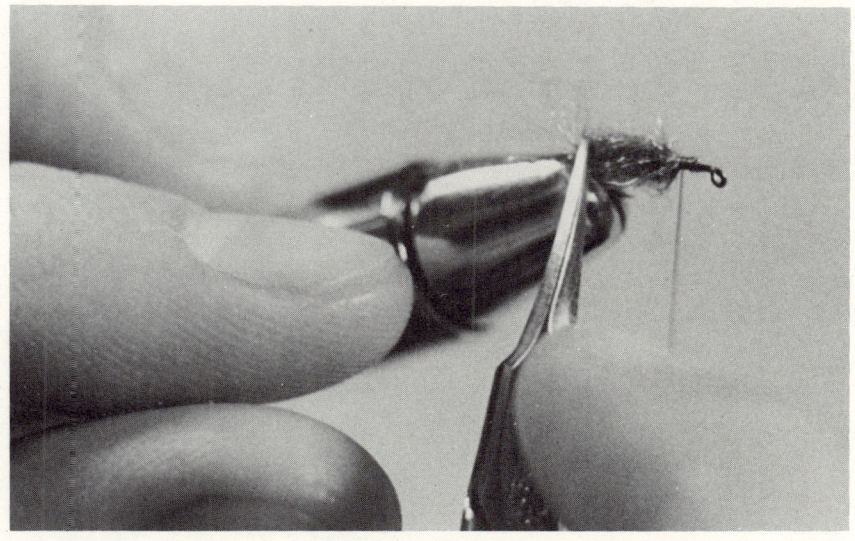

10
With a scissors point, pull free some of the filaments of the overbody so that they dangle off the back, representing the loosening sheath of the emerging pupa.

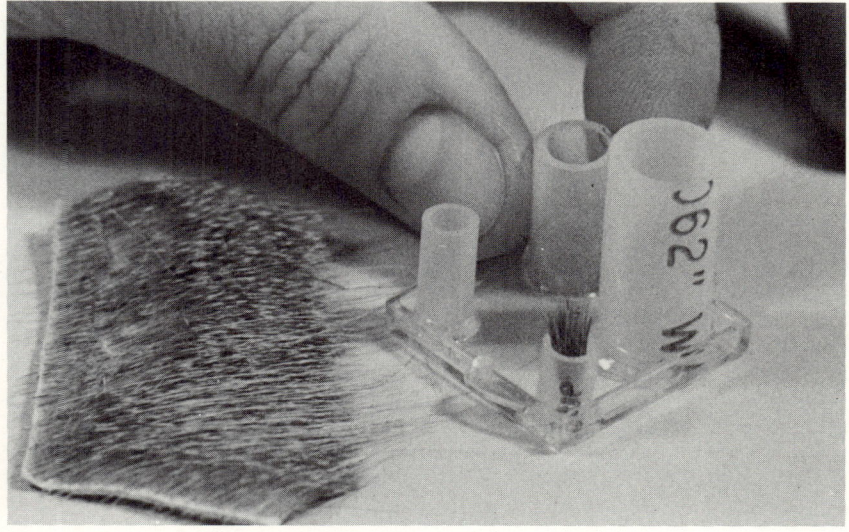

11
For the wing, clip deer hairs from the skin and level the tips in a hair tamper.

12

Tie the short and stubby hair on top of the hook shank. This not only represents the budding wings of an adult caddis but also provides buoyancy to anchor the fly in the surface film.

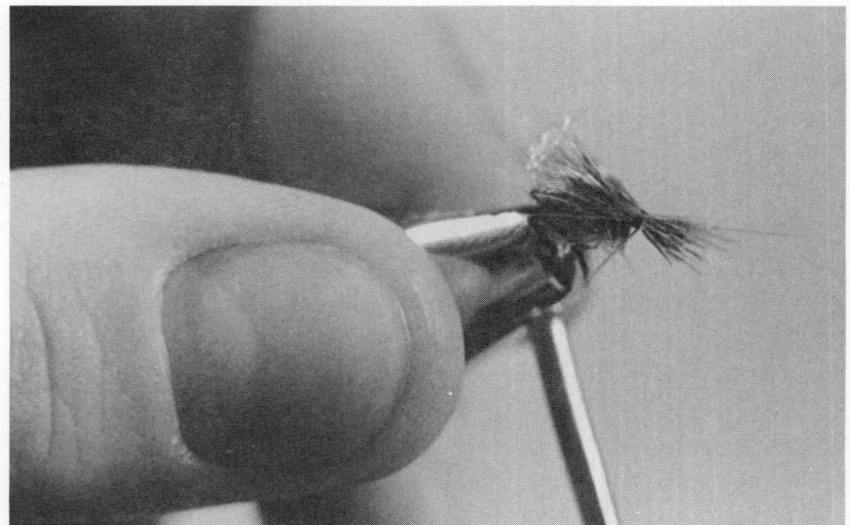

13

To form the head of the pattern, strip four or five marabou fibers from a stalk and tie them over the clipped butts of the wing.

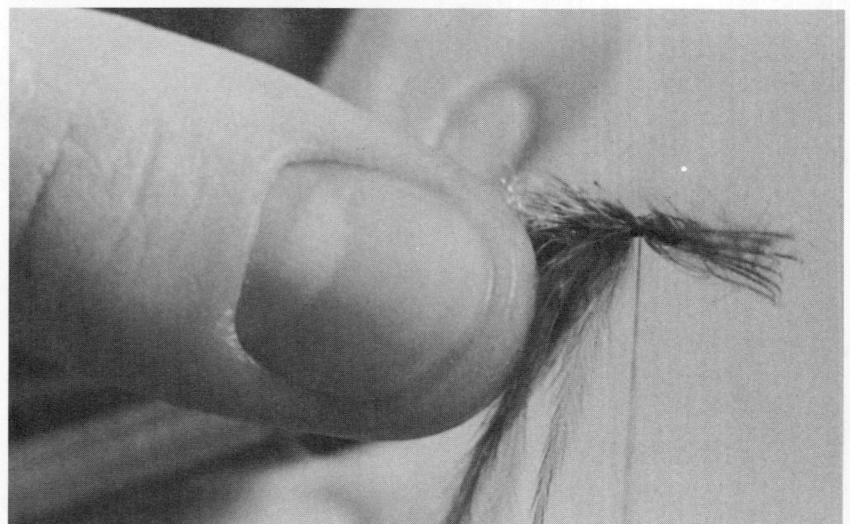

14

Wrap the marabou fibers to the eye of the hook and tie off.

15
Whip-finish to complete fly.

The Robber Fly
By CHAUNCEY K. LIVELY
Photographs by C. K. Lively

In the insect world, robber flies are fearsome bullies. Extremely predaceous, the adults feed on flying insects and are known to attack and capture specimens larger than themselves, like dragonflies. Robber flies are members of a family of which there are said to be 3,000 species, and the range in their appearance is extremely broad. Some are thickset and hairy, resembling bees, but the more common forms are elongate, roughly approximating damselflies.

The robber fly our pattern represents is a relatively large insect with a conspicuous abdomen tapering to a point, a hairy thorax and head, and prominent legs and wings which fold flat over the back at rest. They are apparently attracted to water by the presence of aquatic insects and, strangely, they often seem to deliberately alight on the water, where they drift with wings extended at an angle. Trout react to them with a vengeance, taking them in eruptive rises reminiscent of grasshopper time.

Although the prevalence of robber flies is widespread, particularly in wooded areas, we began to notice them in quantity on the Au Sable River in Michigan and it was there that the Robber Fly pattern was developed. In the past ten years or so I have used the pattern with great success on a wide variety of streams, both freestone and limestone, and it is now one of my favorite terrestrials. The Robber Fly seems to do its best work during daylight hours in hot weather, when the naturals are on the wing, although I've caught many trout on the pattern as early as mid-May and as late as October. Fish it along obvious cover and twitch it occasionally to suggest life.

MATERIALS

THREAD: 7/0 Herb Howard's brown, prewaxed and black nymph
HOOK: size 14 regular shank, fine wire
ABDOMEN: tan elk (preferred) or deer body hair
THORAX: peacock herl
WINGS: fine-textured deer body hair with barred tips
HACKLES: one each, medium brown and grizzly

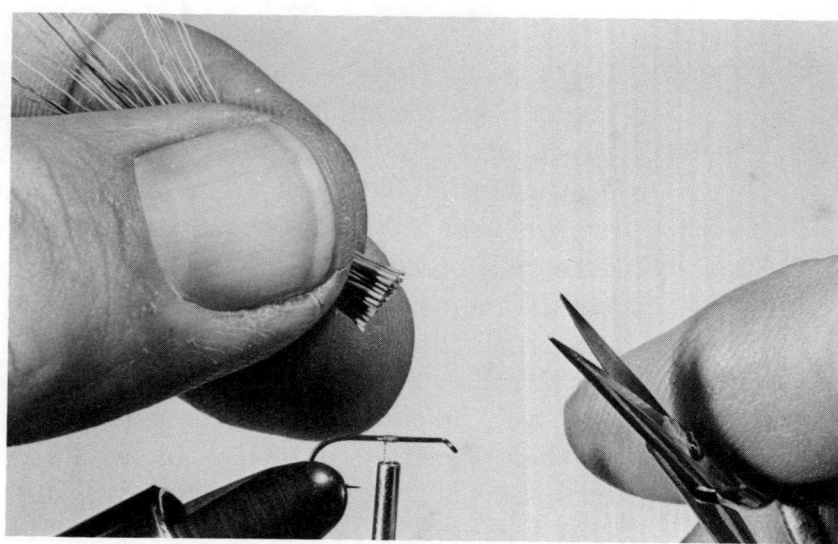

1
Clamp a size 14 dry fly hook in the vise and tie in a brown, prewaxed 7/0 thread at the center of the shank. Cut a bunch of elk body hair close to the hide and stroke or comb out fuzz and short hairs. Then trim the butts evenly. When pressed flat, the hair should be about ¼ inch wide at the butts.

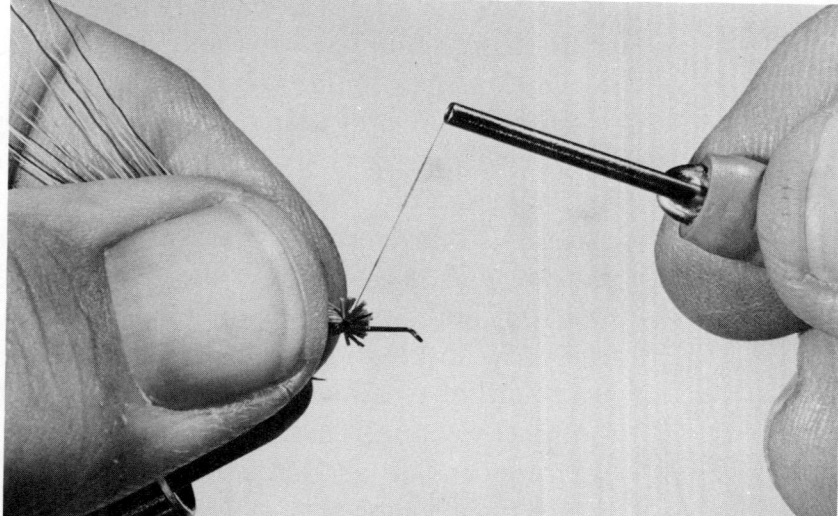

2
Hold the hair in a rocker grip over tie-in point, with about ⅛ inch of the butts projecting toward the eye. Then make a firm, steady turn of thread around hair and shank, causing the hair butts to flare. Still maintaining the tension, make a second turn.

3
Without slackening the tension, wind forward through the flared butts and back again, binding down the individual butts. Half-hitch.

4
Stroke the hair to remove any slack and arrange it in a bundle. Hold the hair in place with the left hand and, with the right, make spaced turns of thread, simulating body segments. To do this, you will have to pass the bobbin underneath the left hand and over the vise, but you may manipulate your left forefinger to hold each turn in place as you progress. Decrease the width of the segments as you work toward the end of the abdomen and increase the thread tension to achieve a tapered effect. When you have wrapped a distance roughly equivalent to the length of the shank, make an extra turn of thread over the last and reverse directions, wrapping back to the hook over the previous winds in a crossing pattern.

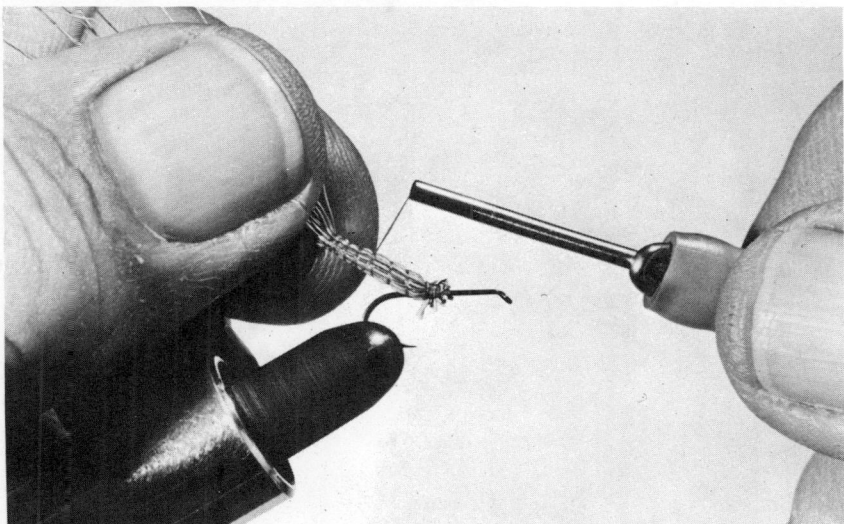

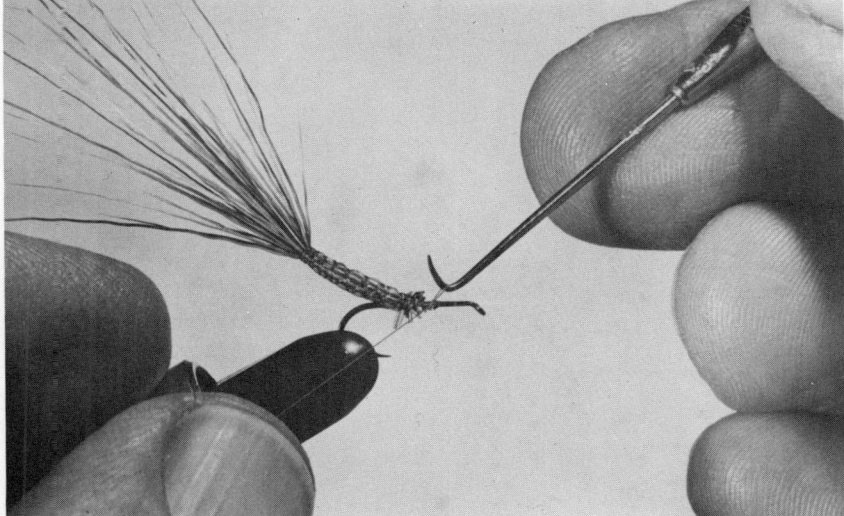

5
Wind the thread to the bare shank ahead of the hair, whip-finish, and cut the thread close to the hook. You are now finished with the brown thread.

6
Remove the hook from the vise and trim the unbound hair to a sharp taper. The finished abdomen should be about as long as the overall length of the hook, from the outside of the eye to the outside of the bend. Also trim off any stubble of hair butts.

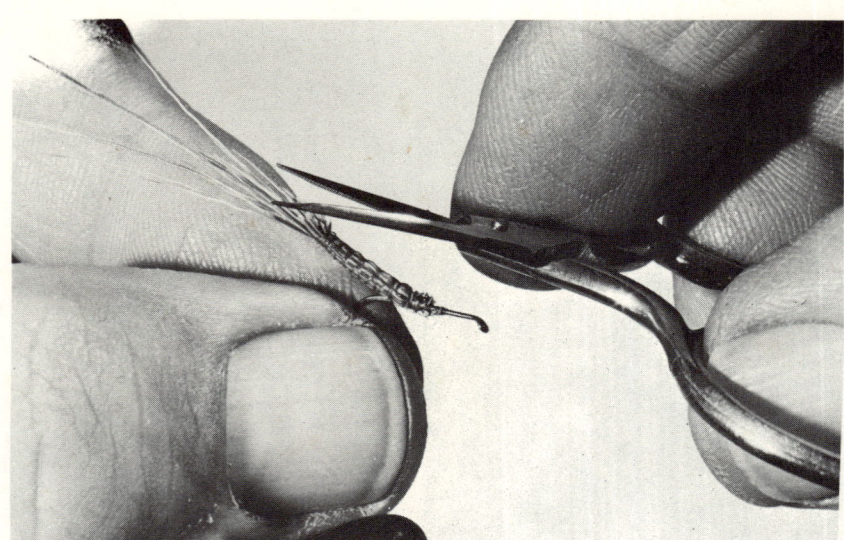

7
Replace the hook in the vise and tie in the black nymph thread over the previous whip finish. Wind the thread back to the base of the abdomen and allow it to hang under weight. Select three peacock herls and tie in by the tips underneath the abdomen. Trim off excess tips. For added durability, wind the herls around the thread for a length of about 3 inches.

8
Wind a thorax of the entwined herl and tie off, allowing plenty of space behind the eye for wings and hackle. Trim excess herl.

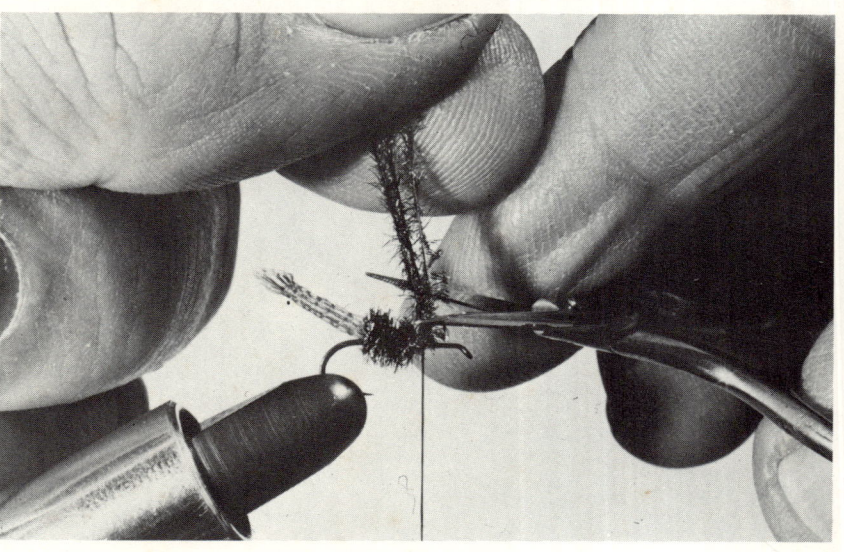

9

For wings, cut a bunch of fine-textured deer body hair with barred tips and remove the fuzz. Match the tips evenly, either with a hair tamper or manually, and bind to the top of the shank in front of the thorax. The tips of the hair should extend nearly to the end of the abdomen. Trim waste hair butts.

10

Separate the hair with a bodkin needle into equal halves and wind the thread between them in figure-8 turns, positioning the wings along the sides at an angle. Then apply a drop of lacquer to the base of each wing, as shown.

11

Select a medium-brown and a grizzly hackle of dry-fly quality, with barbules about twice as long as the gap of the hook. Hold the hackles together and strip off the webby lower barbules. Leaving a small gap in front of wings, tie the hackles in together with figure-8 turns of thread, positioning them perpendicular to the shank, on the edge, with the dull sides facing the eye. Then bend the stems forward along the shank and bind with three tight turns. Trim waste stems. (If the foregoing appears contrary to normal practice, consider these advantages: tied in thus, the hackles are in perfect position for the first turns, with their stronger planes opposing the forces of air resistance in casting and of surface tension in pickup. And they are locked securely in place without requiring the trimming of short stubs along the stems.) At this point the lacquer applied to the base of the wings should be partially set, in which case, squeeze with tweezers to flatten wings.

12

Clamp hackle pliers to the tip of the rear hackle and wind forward, tying off behind the eye. Then wind the second hackle through the first, rocking the pliers back and forth to avoid depressing the hackle already wound. Tie off and trim waste hackle tips. Wind a fairly large head of thread and whip-finish. Then remove any unused thread and apply head lacquer.

13

Finally, cut a V from the hackle underneath the fly.

14

The finished Robber Fly.

The Two-Feather May
By JOHN F. McKIM
Photographs by Joan McKim

Judged on esthetic merit alone, the Two-Feather May is a winner. Majestically riding the currents, it is a pretty sight to see — fortunately for those of us to whom the usual size 16 hook is invisible. Its popularity among the trout population helps to explain why this dry fly is a standard with many Western fly addicts, including The Old Grouch.

Delicate, yet durable and a good floater, the Two-Feather May is also easy to tie. Endless size and color combinations are possible to match any hatch. In fact, Dick Alf of Sun Valley, Idaho, popularized the fly in the 1960s as the "Hatch Master," although the basic pattern was probably not originated by him. It produces well on slow-moving waters, such as Silver Creek in Idaho.

It is tied with either a spun or a parachute hackle. The original tie was parachute style and I prefer it that way. To me, the fly presents a more natural silhouette and displays superior floating qualities. Use any curved breast or side feather similar to mallard for the tail-body-wing, one that's symmetrical about the stem with fibers equal to body plus wing length. Dyed feathers, offering wider latitude in color, are popular.

MATERIALS

HOOK: sizes 10–18, turned-up eye, 5 extra-short shank
TAIL-BODY-WING: one mallard feather, side or breast
HACKLE: ginger or grizzly are the most popular
THREAD: sizes 4/0–8/0, black or color to match body

1
Choose a nicely curved mallard feather with opposing fibers of equal length. Trim out the tip section. The last fiber on each side will be the tail.

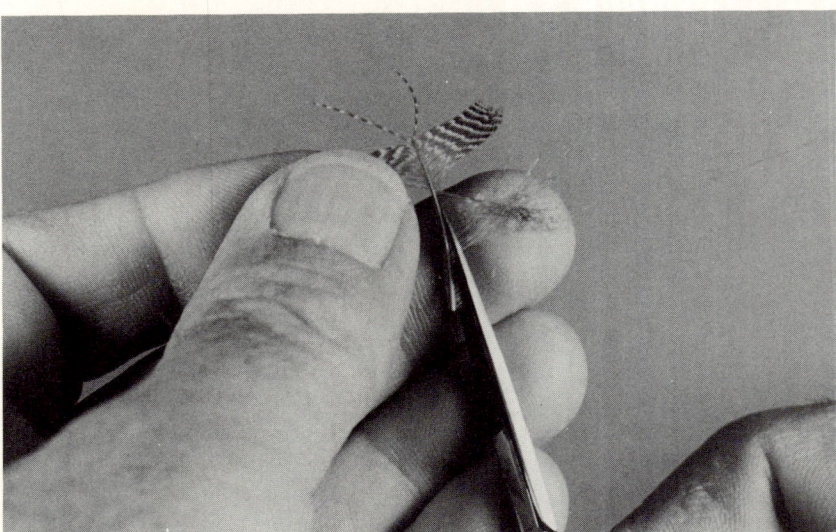

2
Trim off the fibers each side of the stem, leaving ¼-inch fiber segments near the tails.

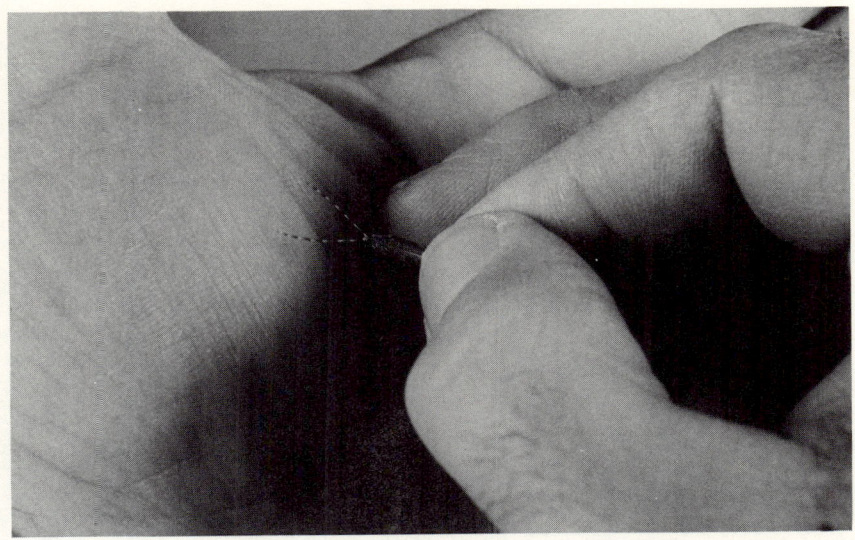

3

Form the body by stroking the remaining fibers forward against the stem. It helps to moisten them with your mouth or wet fingers.

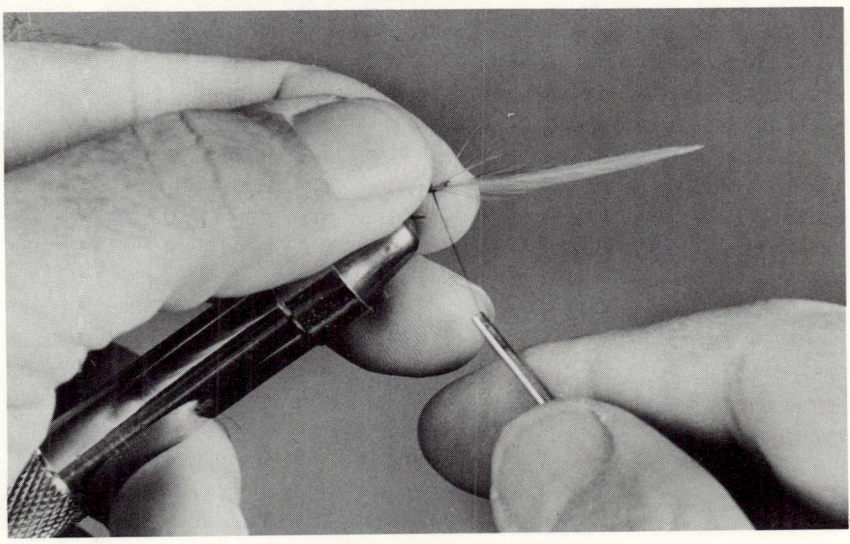

4

Choose a dry hackle with fiber lengths equal to the distance from head to barb. Trim the fibers near the butt, leaving short stubs. Tie concave side down. Leave head space.

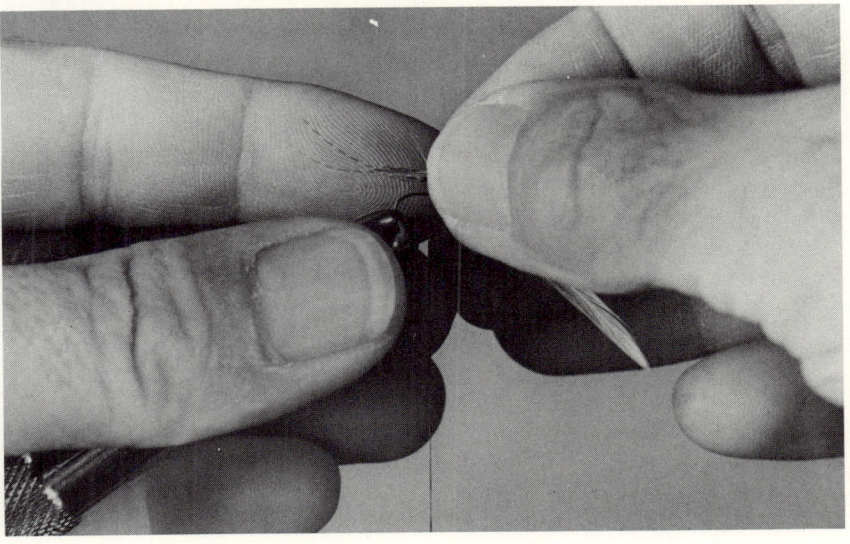

5

Place the body feather squarely on top of the hook. Tie in where the hackle is tied. The body should extend about ¼ inch. The forward-extending fiber tips will become the wings.

6

Raise and trim off the excess stem close to the hook.

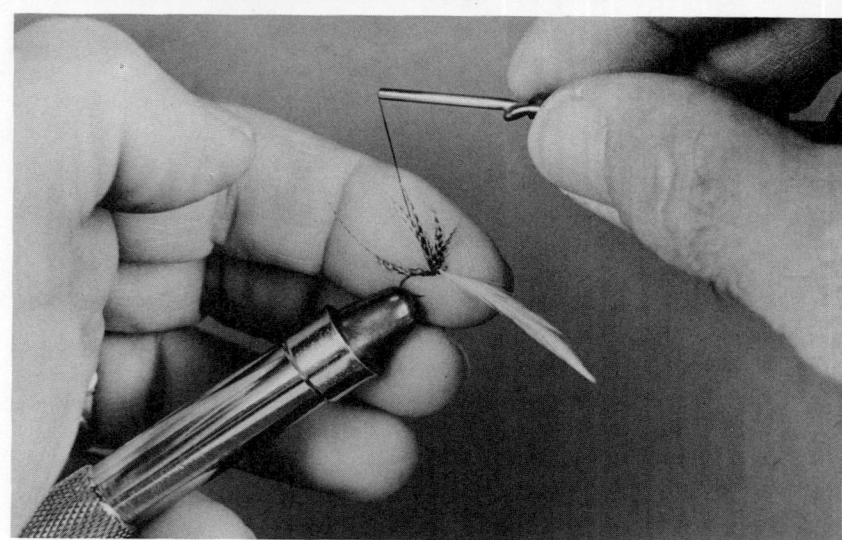

7

To form the wing, lift the mallard fiber tips to the upright position and tie them into place.

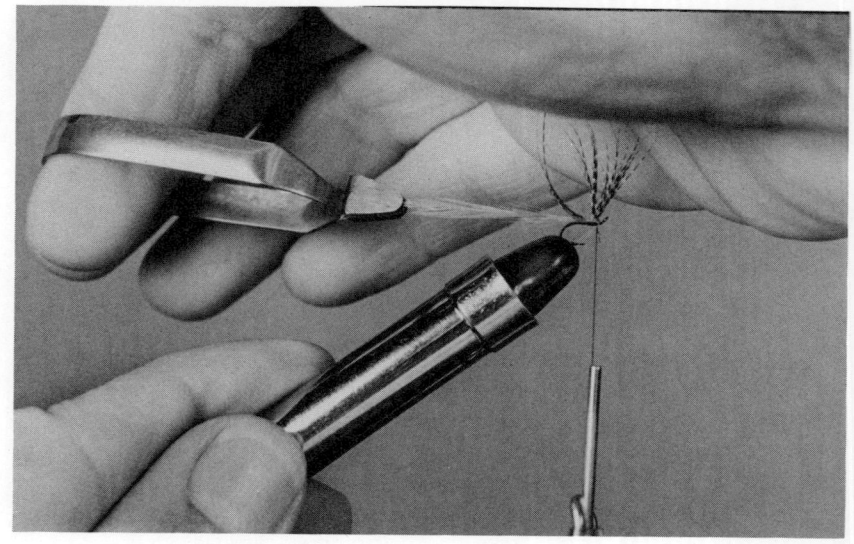

8

With hackle pliers, spin the hackle horizontally under the body and around the base of the wing.

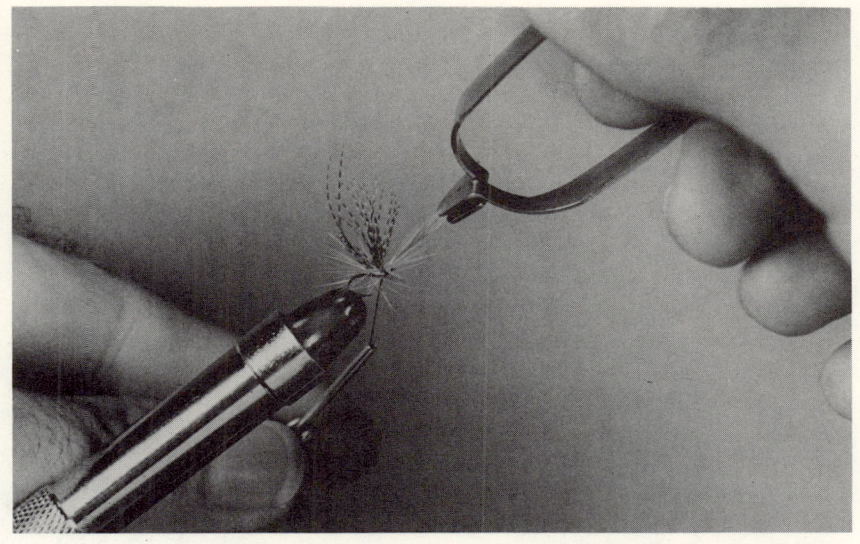

9

Make at least three turns, then tie off the hackle in front of the wing.

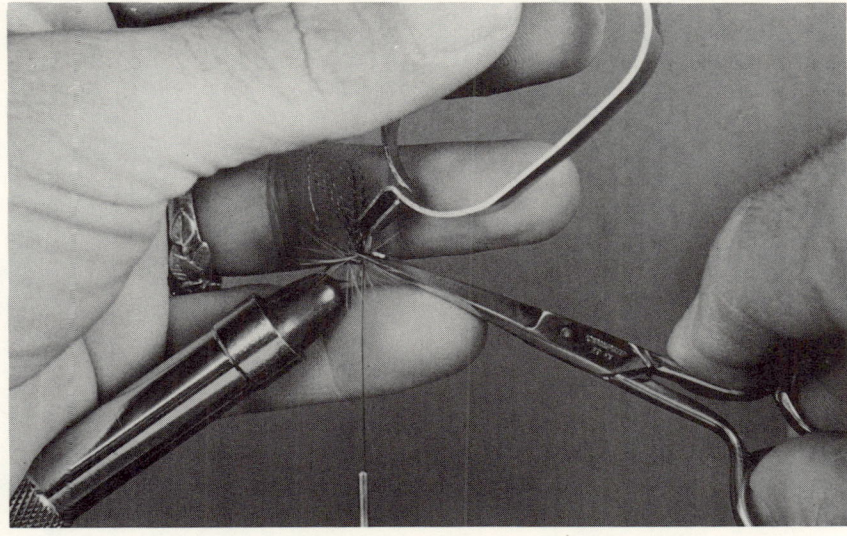

10

After the hackle is secured in place, half-hitch and trim off the excess tip.

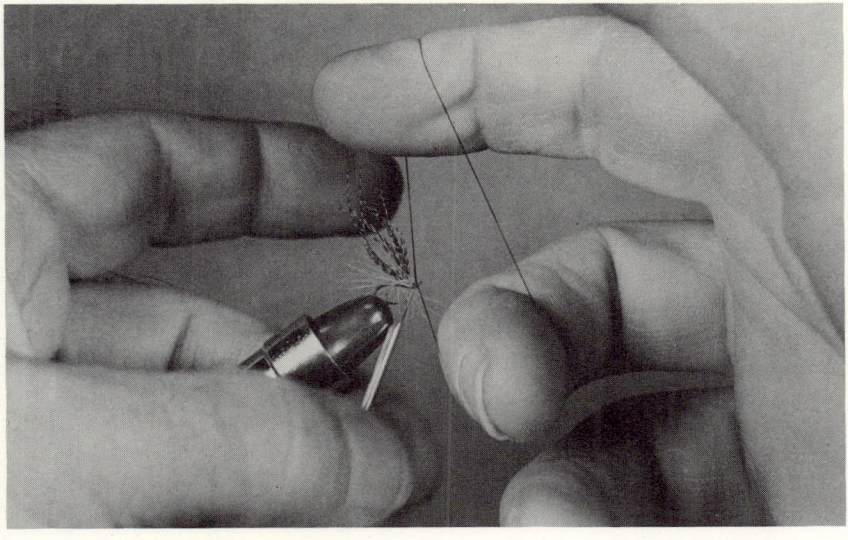

11

Whip-finish a very small head. Three turns are sufficient.

12

Clip the tying thread and use your bodkin to separate and arrange the hackle fibers.

13

Apply thinned cement to the head. Thinned cement spreads into the base of the wing and hackle to make a more durable fly.

14

As the cement dries, use the bodkin to arrange the hackle fibers.

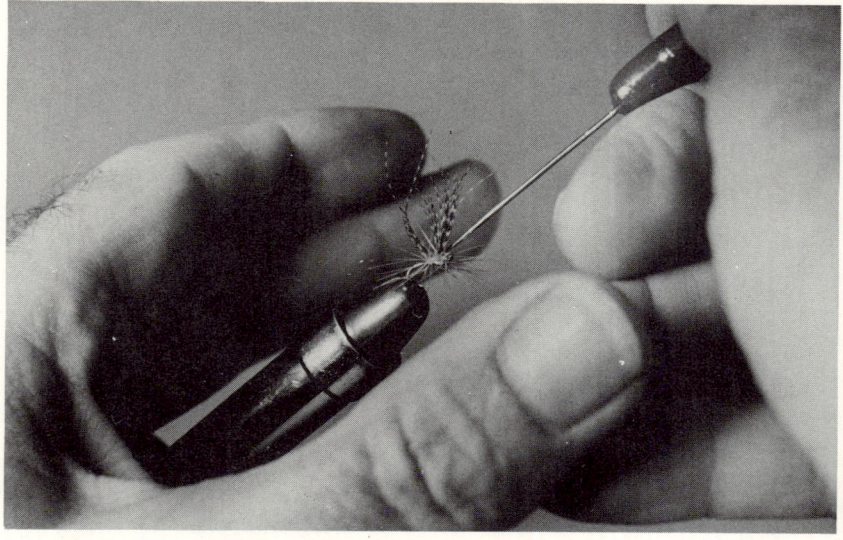

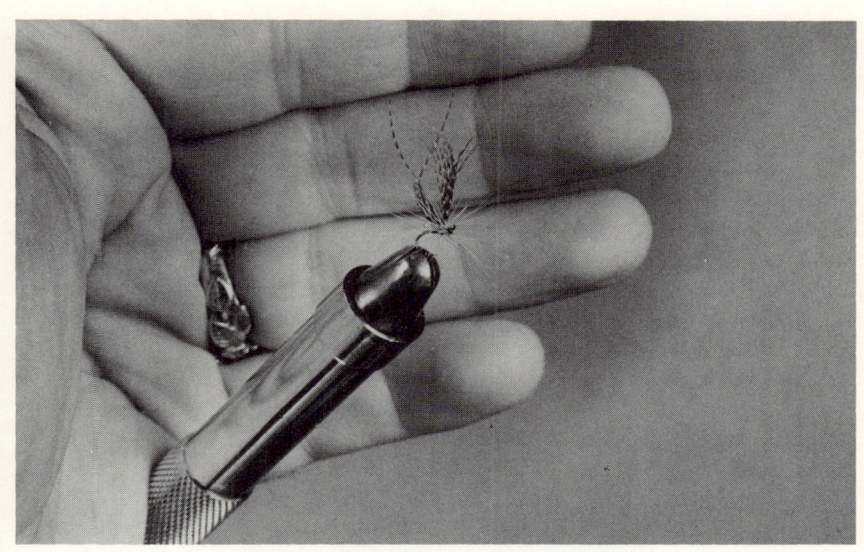

15
Be sure to clean the eye of dried head cement, and the fly is finished.

9

The Marabou Dragon Nymph
By JOHN MERWIN
Photographs by John Merwin

My three-year-old daughter was in hysterics. The big nymph that I'd taken from the pond and thrown into her jar of tadpoles was eating *her* baby toads, and nothing would do but for me to get him out of there. This dragonfly nymph was about an inch long, big enough to inflict a painful bite on an adult's finger, and I carefully lifted it out with a pair of tweezers. The tadpoles have hatched and the little toads taken back to their pond several months ago, but the nymph sits on my desk yet, carefully preserved in a solution of ethyl alcohol.

Dragonfly nymphs prefer the clean waters — still or flowing, depending on the species — that most people associate with ideal trout habitat, and the nymphal stages of one or more species within this family (Anisoptera) are found in at least some portions of most trout waters around the country. The nymphs of some of the larger forms may require three or more years to mature, at which time they crawl from the water's edge out on a twig or blade of grass where the actual emergence as a winged adult takes place. There are no hatches of dragonflies, such as one associates with mayflies or caddis, nor do there appear to be any mass shoreward migrations of nymphs such as characterize the behavior of the closely related damselflies.

The nymphs represent a food form that is only occasionally available to trout in most areas, yet one large enough to be recognized and taken greedily. Unfortunately, very little has appeared about these nymphs in popular angling literature, although you can find an excellent chapter on them in Ernest Schwiebert's *Nymphs* (Winchester, 1973).

Observation of my tadpole-eating specimen, along with others over the years, has shown certain key characteristics of the insect's body configuration that I subsequently incorporated into the Marabou Dragon: an ovoid, flattened abdomen, terminating in a series of short, sharply pointed "tails," a narrow, round thorax, and a broad, flat head with very prominent eyes. One other characteristic of note: the nymph bodies are often covered with short, fine hairs, which, as the nymph rests quietly on the bottom for the most part, catch the silt in its aquatic environment and also promote the growth of various types of algae on its back. When the insect moves around or floats in the current, these hairs wave back and forth in a manner that is *exactly* duplicated by the marabou from which the body of this imitation is made. Here's the pattern; vary the colors to match those nymphs that you've been able to locate in your own waters.

Burr's Brite

Ted's Crayfish

The Matuka Sculpin

The Pre-emerger Nymph

 The Cotton-Thread Stonefly Nymph
 The Emergent Caddis Pupa
 The Robber Fly

 The Two-Feather May

The Marabou Dragon Nymph

The Adult Stone Fly

The Flat-Wing Fly

The Hair-Wing Matuka

Vinny's Midge

The Cardinelle

The Painted Lady

MATERIALS

HOOK: Mustad #9575, sizes 2–8, bent to shape

UNDERBODY: thin cardboard, cut to basic body shape and epoxied to hook shank, and floss of a color to match dubbing

TAILS: four short fibers of stripped goose

RIBBING: flat monofilament, color to match dubbing

BODY: marabou of appropriate color, chopped, then dubbed

WING CASE: dark turkey (or same dyed to appropriate color), lacquered and trimmed to deep V-shape

LEGS: Ambroid cement bubbles (see captions)

THREAD: 6/0 silk (nylon, especially prewaxed nylon, won't work as well because the adhesives used for this fly adhere to it poorly)

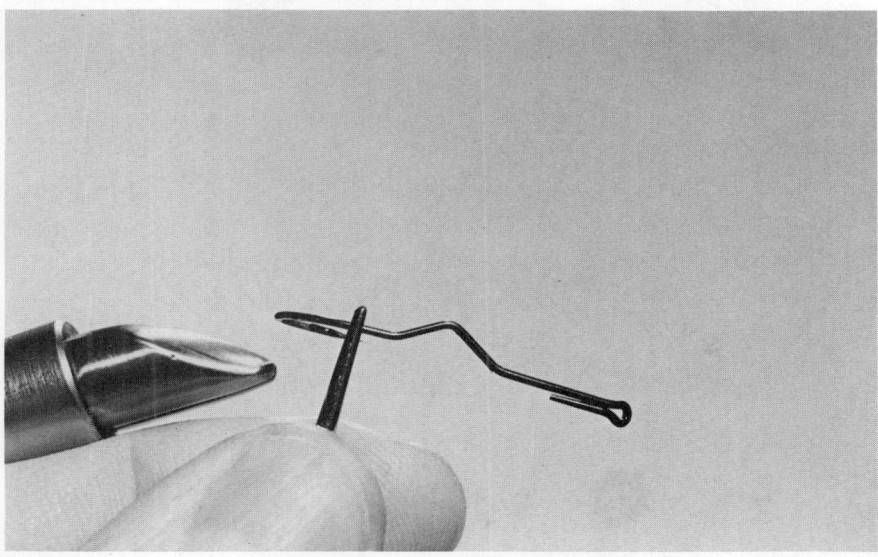

1
Use a pair of long-nosed pliers to bend the hook shank as shown. The bend will prevent the underbody from rotating on the shank.

2
Cut a piece of thin, stiff cardboard (paper matchbook covers work well) to the characteristic body shape of the dragonfly nymph. I use a template (cut from thin plastic) to trace a quantity of them so I can easily make a large number at one sitting.

3

Tie the cardboard body flat on top of the hook shank. Tie off the thread with a whip finish and then smear epoxy along the bottom. Be sure to fill the entire space along both sides of the hook shank, covering the entire bottom thoroughly. I put a number of these on a sheet of aluminum foil as I go along, then bake them all in the kitchen stove at about 175° for an hour or until the epoxy is completely cured.

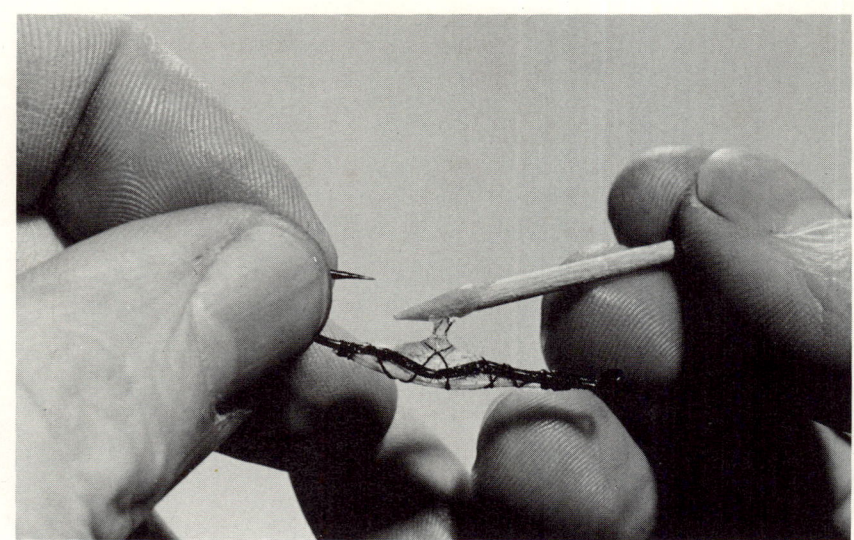

4

Wind some dubbed marabou at the rear of the hook shank to form a small, tight ball. This will support the tails and will also prevent subsequent materials from slipping off the rear of the body.

5

Use four broad fibers of stripped goose for tails.

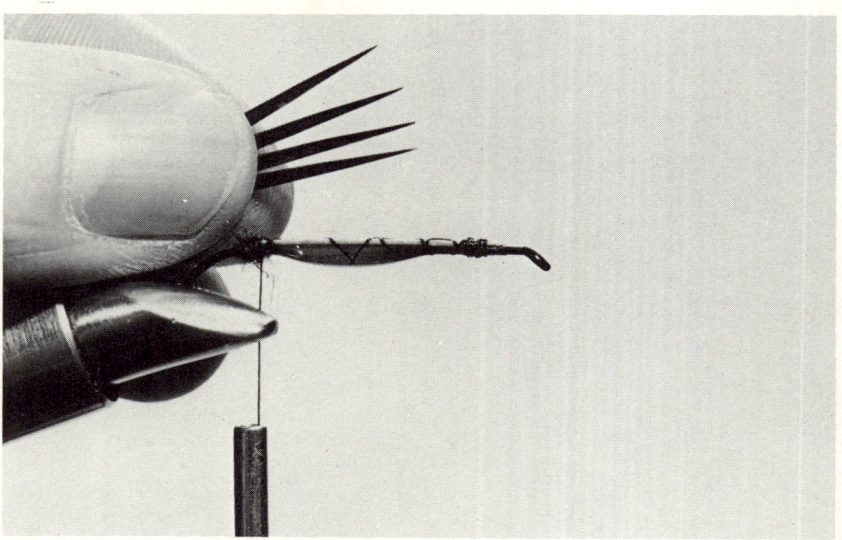

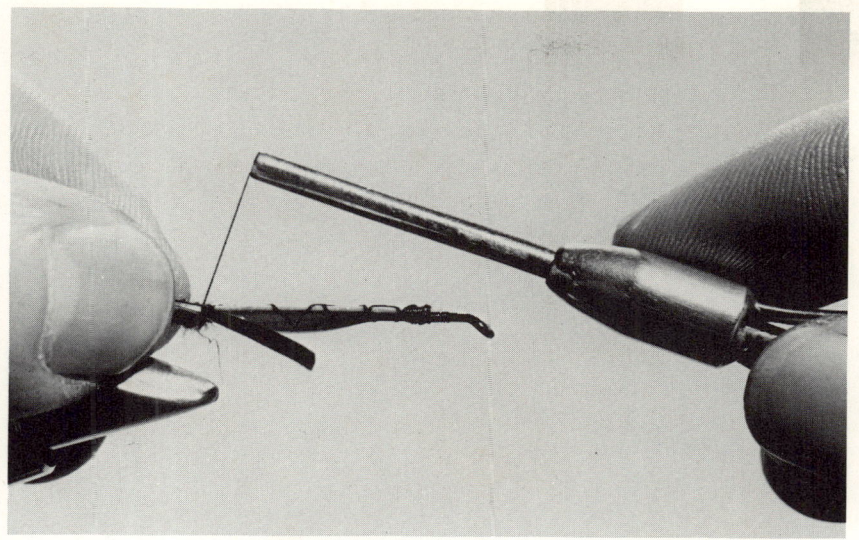

6

Tie in each goose fiber directly forward of the ball. Make sure the tails are distributed evenly around the top and sides of the ball and not all bunched together. When finished, the tails should all be about ¼ inch long.

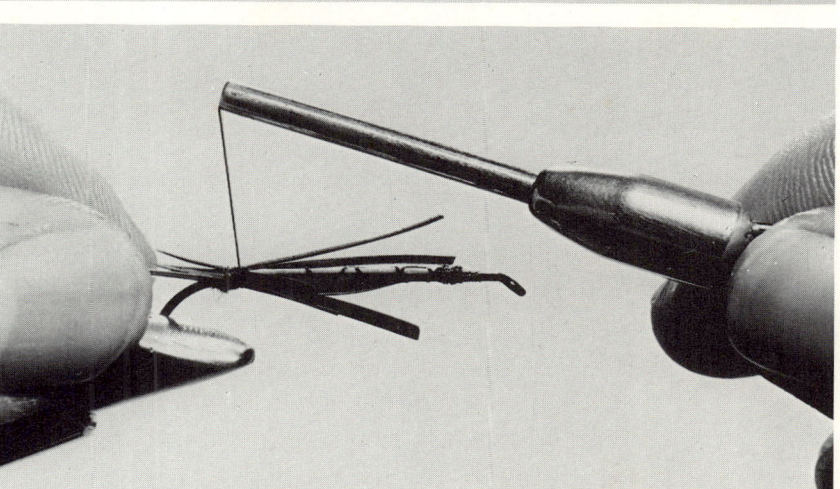

7

When all four tails have been tied in, tie in the brown, flat monofilament ribbing.

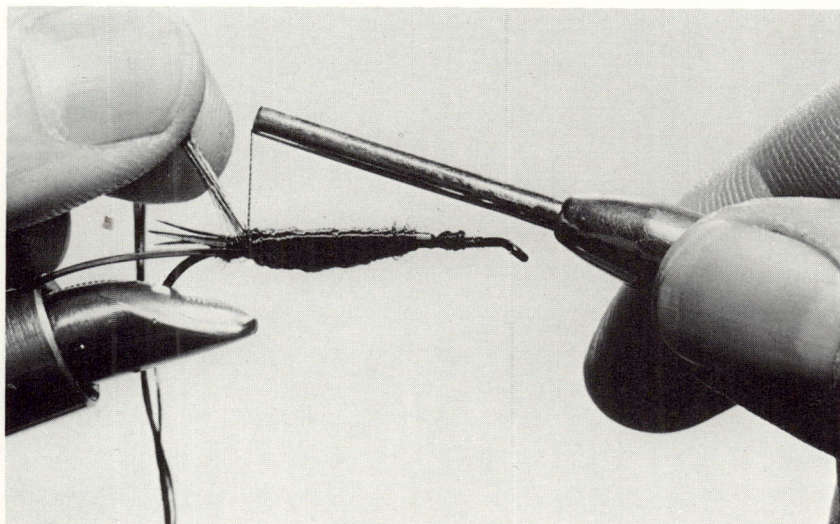

8

Enlarge the underbody with three or four layers of floss of the same color as the rest of the fly. Make sure that the floss doesn't extend to the forward third of the hook shank.

9

Starting from the rear, dub a fuzzy marabou body, once again stopping at the forward third of the hook shank.

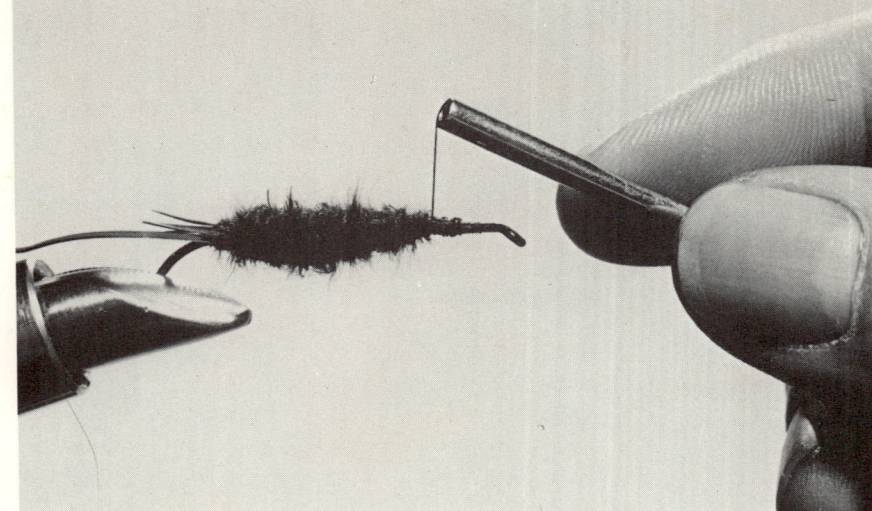

10

Rib with six or seven turns of monofilament. The fly is now ready for its legs, in this case, fibers of stripped goose with a simple overhand knot tied in each fiber. An unknotted and a knotted fiber are shown.

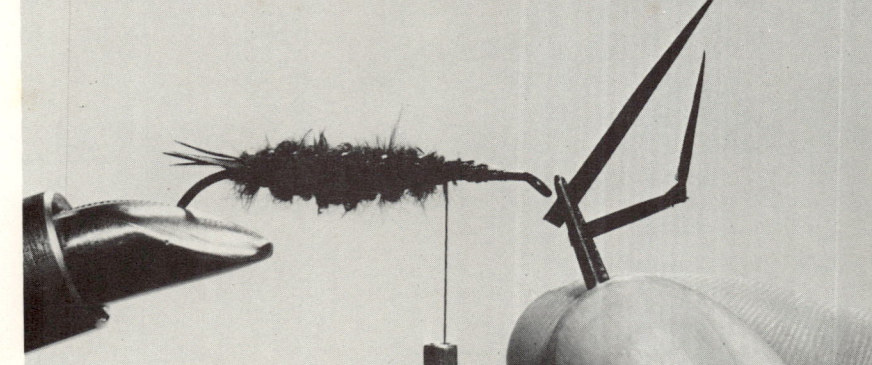

11

Tie in the first pair of legs with a figure-8 wrap at the base of each. (For clarity, the rest of the procedure is viewed from the top of the fly.)

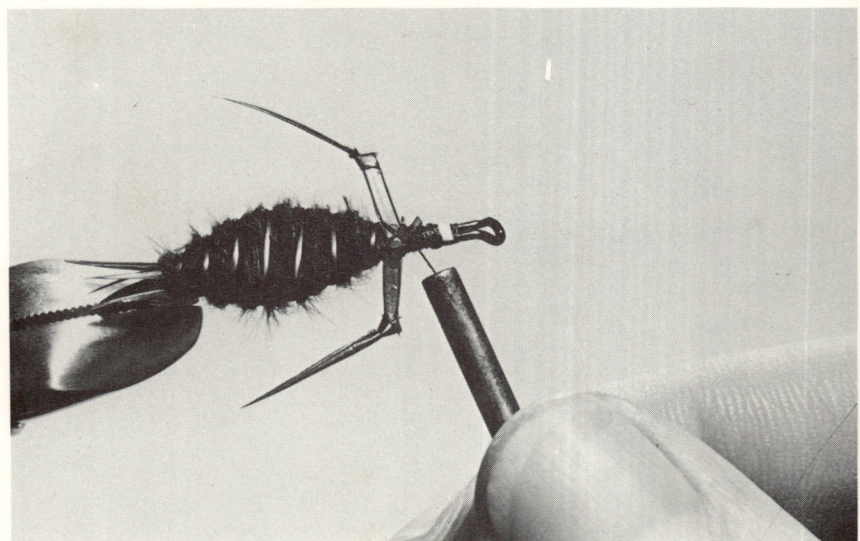

12

Tie in the remaining legs until all six are in position, determining the angle at which each will project from the hook shank. A little practice will make this seemingly complicated process go very quickly. Stripped goose is both smooth-surfaced and strong, and thus tends to slide around after being tied in. I coat the leg bases with Super Glue at this point to hold them more firmly.

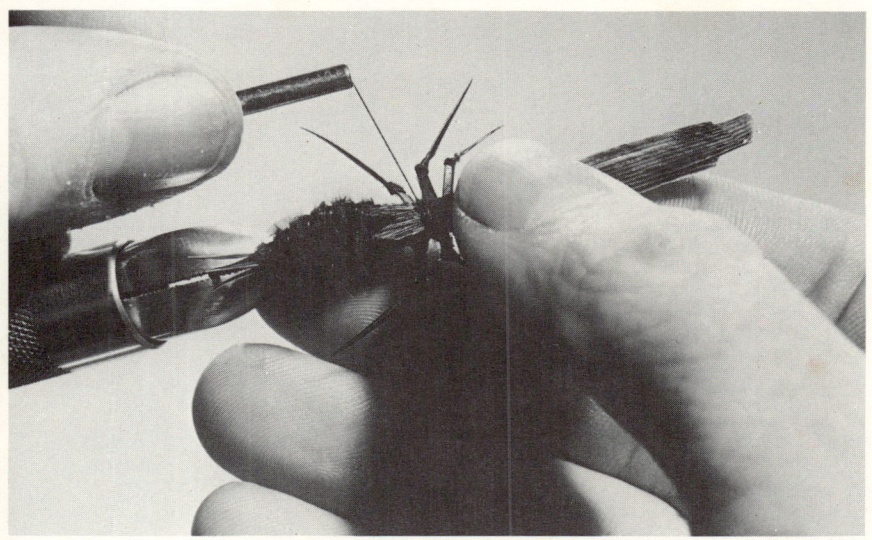

13

Apply a *little* dubbing around the bases of the first leg pair, then tie in a wing case of lacquered dark-brown turkey tail that has been cut to a deep V-shape.

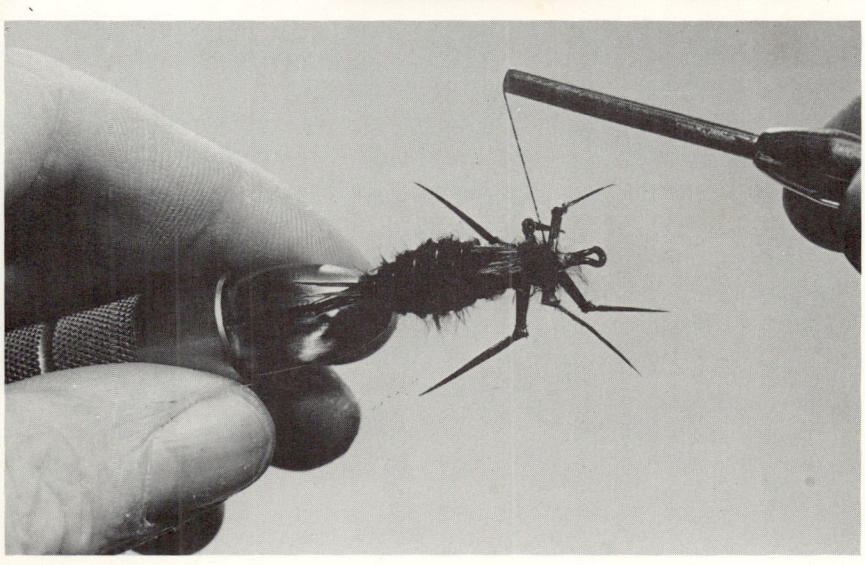

14

Wrap dubbed marabou sparingly around the next two leg pair bases. The pressure of the dubbing should angle all of the legs slightly downward.

15

Now for the eyes. Once again, these should be made in substantial quantity at one sitting rather than as each fly is tied. Using 3X leader material, tie an overhand knot in the end of a number of pieces, each about 4 inches long. Trim one end of the mono close to the knot. I then tape 20–30 of these to a small, round bottle cap so the knotted ends project an equal distance downward. I then can dip all of them in Ambroid cement at one time. Each knot on the end of each strand will hold a droplet of cement. Put the whole assembly into a warm (150°) oven immediately after dipping. Because the outside of the droplet will dry more quickly than the inside, heating the droplets makes them dry as small, hard, *hollow* bubbles. For lighter-colored patterns, they can be used in their natural amber color. For darker flies, I either dip them in black lacquer, as here, or color them with waterproof markers.

16

Tie in the two strands with a figure-8 wrap. After tying in, each end of the mono is pulled, which pulls each eye into position. The free ends of the mono are pulled back toward the rear of the fly, tied off right behind the eyes, and trimmed.

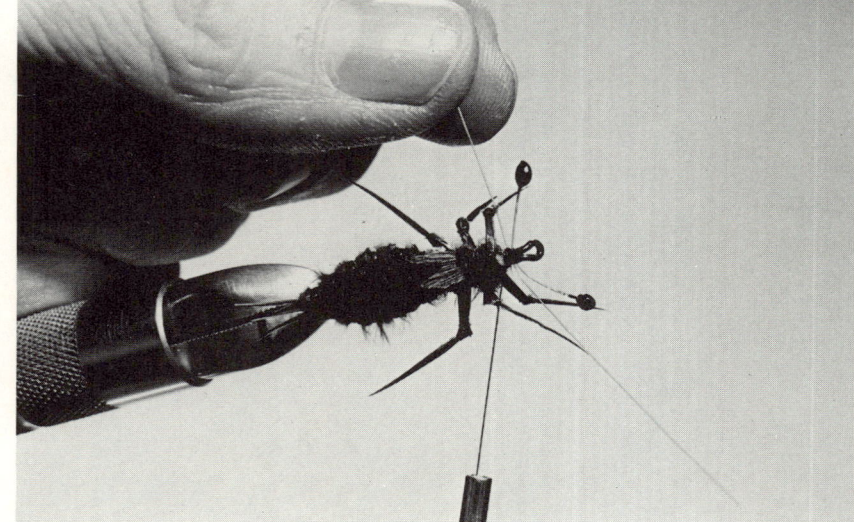

17

Now wind some dubbed marabou behind the eyes and around the eye stalks to produce the nymph's characteristically broad, flat head. Whip-finish in front of the eyes and coat the knot with cement. The finishing knot, if done with care and without excess thread, should be almost invisible.

18
The finished fly.

The Flat-Wing Fly
By SID A. NEFF, JR.
Photographs by S. A. Neff, Jr.

Now that almost everyone has discovered the caddis fly, there is a multiplicity of caddis imitations in the fly shops. The one imitation that has not received the attention I think it deserves is the flat-wing caddis. This is an extremely effective fly on the flat pools of the freestone rivers and on all the limestoners and spring creeks where caddis are found.

The Flat-Wing Fly concept is a design of a fly, rather than a pattern; therefore, its form can be applied to representations of several insects. Besides the various species of adult caddis flies, it can be used to imitate stone flies and, in small sizes, beetles and clusters of ovipositing bibios and chironomids. This type of design portrays the silhouette of the insect rather than the height. By simply altering the shape and length of the wing and changing the color of the other materials, it can be made to imitate a range of insects.

The flat-wing design is not new. I've traced the concept back to the 1880s, when Halford used a pike scale for the wing of a Black Gnat imitation. Several English fly dressers used the flat-wing concept to imitate sedges, beetles, and bibios. During the First World War, Leonard West prescribed covert and breast feathers for flat-wing flies. In the 1930s, J. C. Mottram wrote about dressing sedges and smuts with flat wings and went as far as to trim the feathers to the shape of the natural. The covert or breast feather made a fine-looking wing when dry, but when it got wet, it shriveled up and lost its original shape. In the 1940s, Vincent Marinaro began using jungle cock feathers to imitate leafhoppers and beetles. These feathers held their original shape when wet but there was no choice of colors.

In the early 1960s, I began experimenting with the flat-wing design. When the uncoated wing proved a failure, I tried coating the feathers with head cement. It was an improvement over the uncoated wings, but there were shortcomings. The cement made the wing heavy and brittle, and it would not lie flat on the fly. Then I discovered Pliobond. This rubber solution gave the feather just enough rigidity so that it could be trimmed to a desired shape (something that was difficult with the uncoated feather) and easily glued into position on top of the fly. It is also flexible enough to bend when the fly is taken by the trout. Unlike the brittle cement-covered wing, which breaks up after one or two fish, the flexible wing retains its shape after five or six. The trick is to use a very thin solution and the best is from a tube — lacking that, thin down the solution in the bottle.

The wings of adult caddis flies are fairly opaque and some have dark markings. Breast and back feathers from game birds, such as hen pheasant, woodcock, grouse, and snipe, work well, as do some domestic hens. The wing of the caddis imitations should have a small notch at the rear corresponding to the silhouette of the natural insect. This design is also effective for imitating adult stone flies. The wings of the natural are paler and more translucent than the caddis. I like to use the breast or back feathers from a blue dun hen. When this feather is coated it becomes semi-translucent. The wing of this imitation should be narrower than the caddis fly and rounded on the end instead of notched. For imitating the beetles I find in limestone meadows, I use crow or black or brown bantam feathers.

One of my most successful discoveries was finding that a Flat-Wing Fly with black hackle and a blue dun wing was well received by the trout when the Black Gnat and black Chironomids were ovipositing. Usually several males will gather on one female, creating a "cluster." As the clusters float along they offer a bigger bite than the individuals, and therefore the larger trout look for them. Apparently the light pattern of the cluster imitation is similar to the light pattern of the natural group. During the time these tiny insects are so active, I find little need for any other flies. I dress the clusters on 20s and 22s. Although the Flat-Wing Flies do take trout on broken water, they are at their best on gentle-flowing rivers. Some of the most selective trout I have ever encountered have succumbed to these flies, often in preference to other designs.

MATERIALS

HOOK: Mustad #94840, sizes 12–22

TAIL: none except in the stone fly representation, then two hackle barbs

BODY: fur or a mixture of fur and poly to correspond to the color of the natural insect

WING: breast, back of wing covert feathers coated with a rubber solution and trimmed to the desired shape (color and markings should correspond to the natural insect)

HACKLE: shiny cock to correspond to the legs of the natural insect

THREAD: prewaxed nylon 6/0 (color should match other materials)

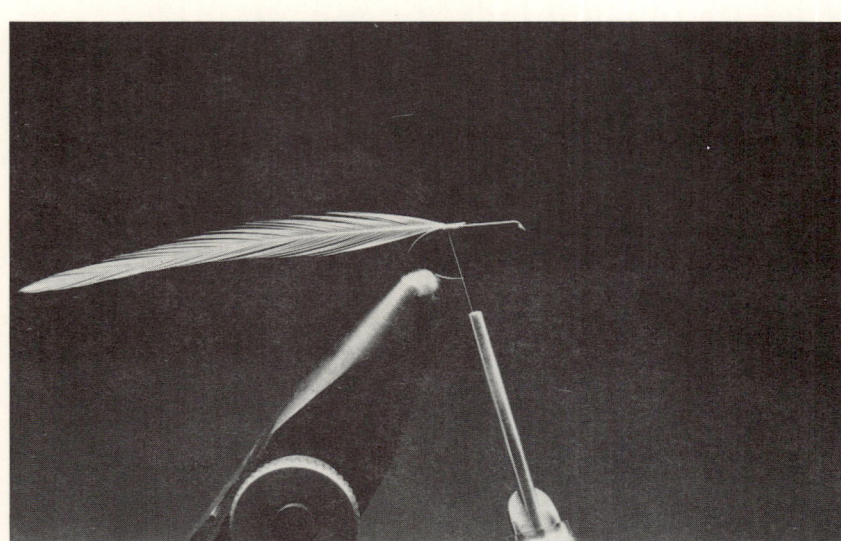

1
Apply the thread to the last third of the hook shank and tie in the hackle (convex side toward the tyer), wrapping toward the bend of the hook.

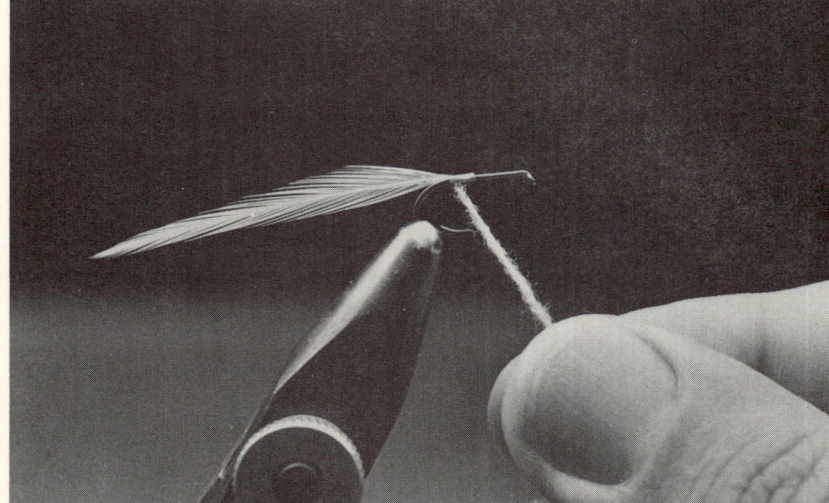

2
Spin the dubbing material onto the thread and wrap it onto the hook to form the body. Leave approximately one-third of the shank of the hook (at the eye) bare.

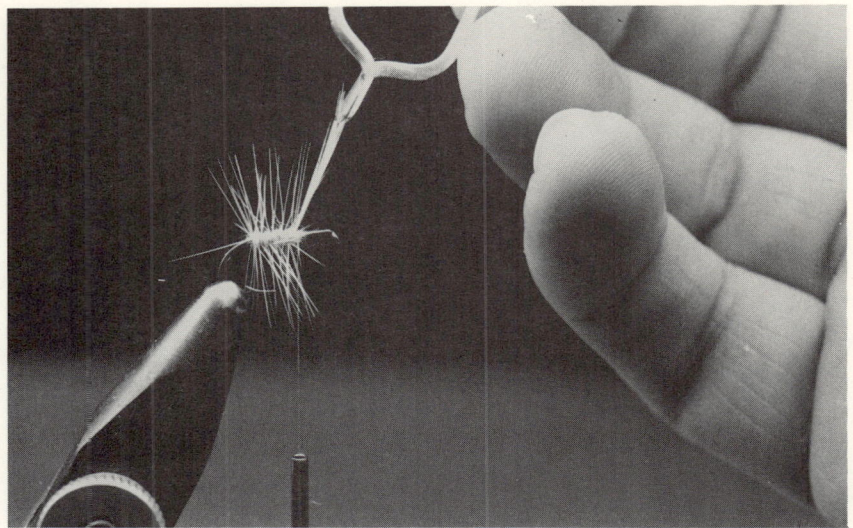

3
Wrap on the hackle, palmer fashion, over the dubbed body.

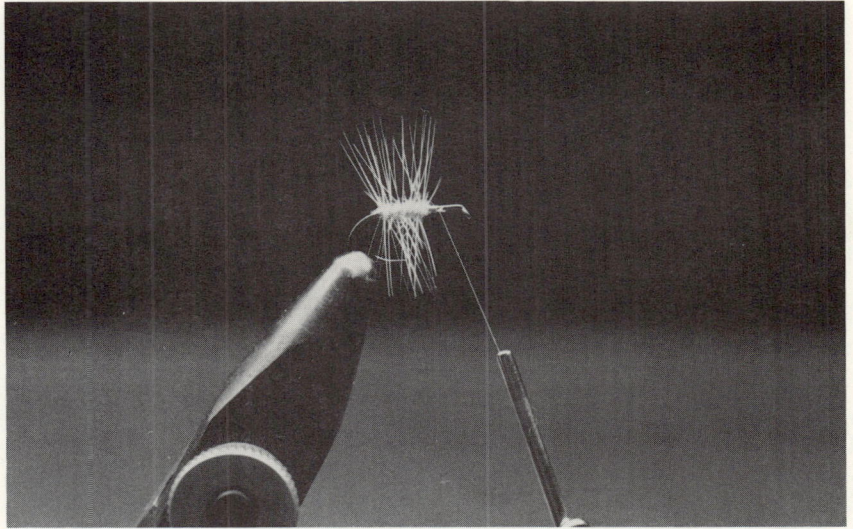

4
Tie off the hackle at the end of the dubbed body.

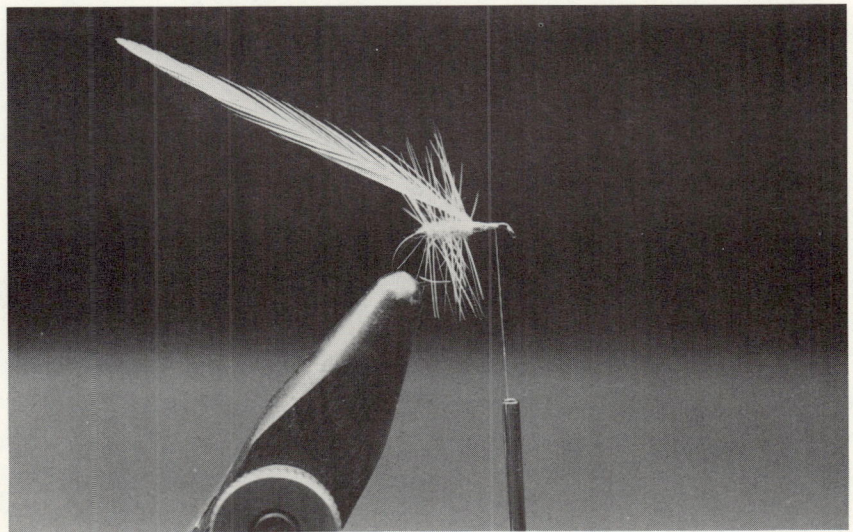

5
Tie in a second hackle (concave side toward the tyer) that is slightly longer than the body hackle.

6
Wrap on the second hackle and tie it off, leaving about 1/16 inch at the eye of the hook (this section of hackle should be thicker than the palmered hackle).

7
Clip the hackle off the top of the fly.

8
After the hackle barbs are clipped off, the remaining hackle on the sides should be flush with the fly's body.

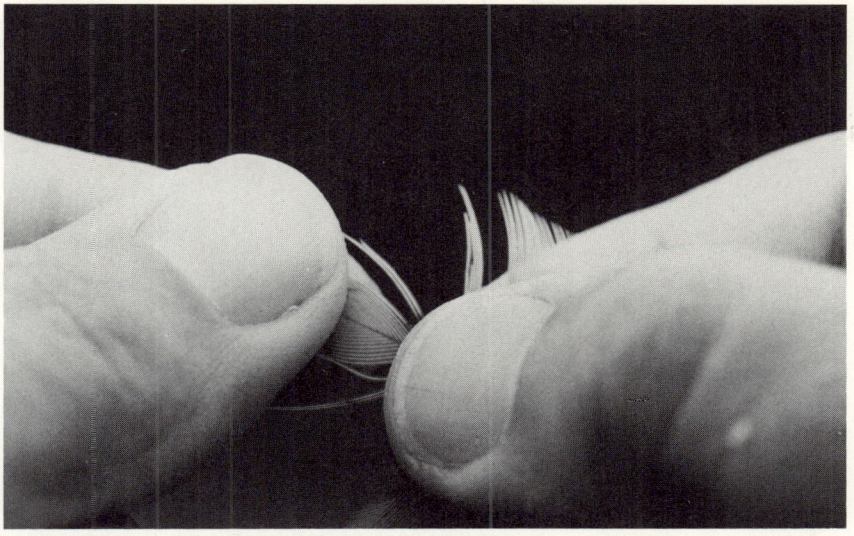

9

Take a breast or back feather and peel away the excess barbs, leaving a section at the end of the feather about one-fourth longer than the finished wing.

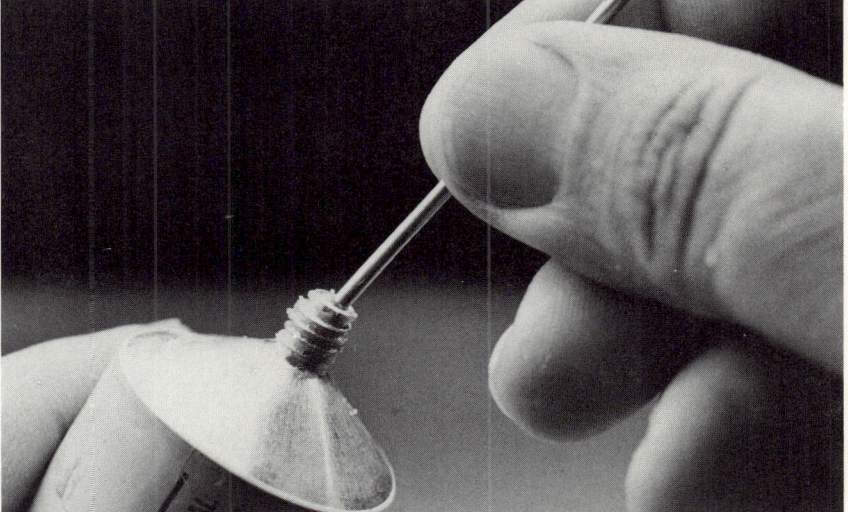

10

Coat the feather with a rubber solution such as contact cement or Pliobond. Solutions that come in tubes tend to be fresher, and therefore thinner, than bottled ones. Insert a needle in the mouth of the tube and gather some of the solution.

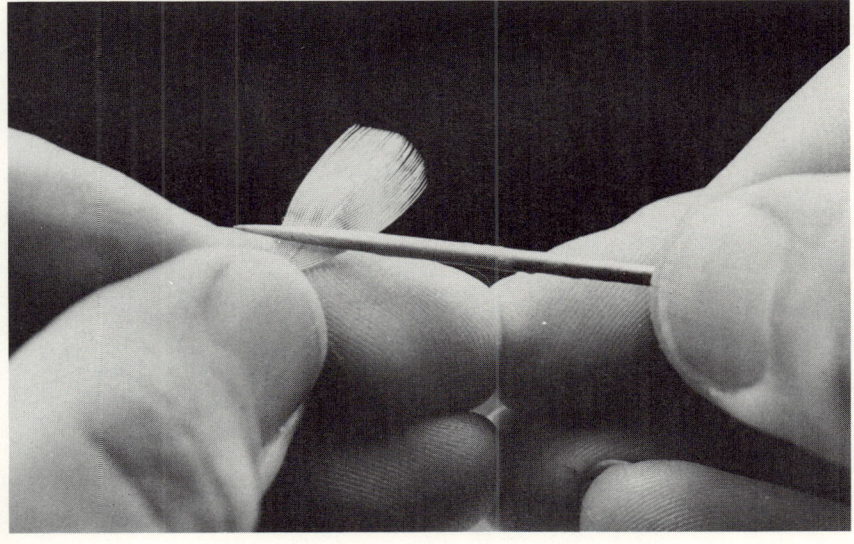

11

As quickly as possible, apply the solution to the *underside* of the feather. The coating should be achieved by drawing the needle along the feather just once. The solution dries very quickly and tends to ball up if more than one coat is applied.

12

After the feather has dried for several minutes, it can be trimmed to the proper shape. Begin by cutting the proper length and then trim the sides.

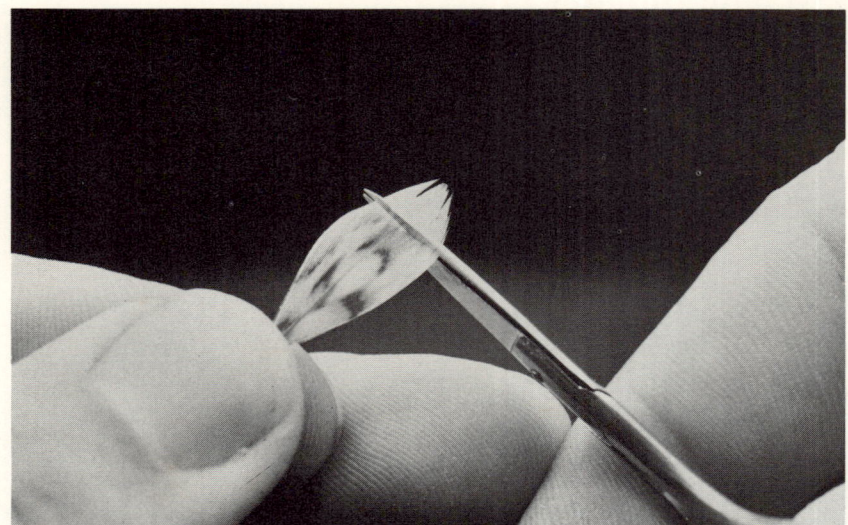

13

In the caddis representations, the wing should be notched as shown, but in the stone fly, beetle, and chironomid representations, it is generally rounded. The wing on the stone fly imitation is longer than the caddis, while the wing on the beetles and chironomids is shorter than the caddis.

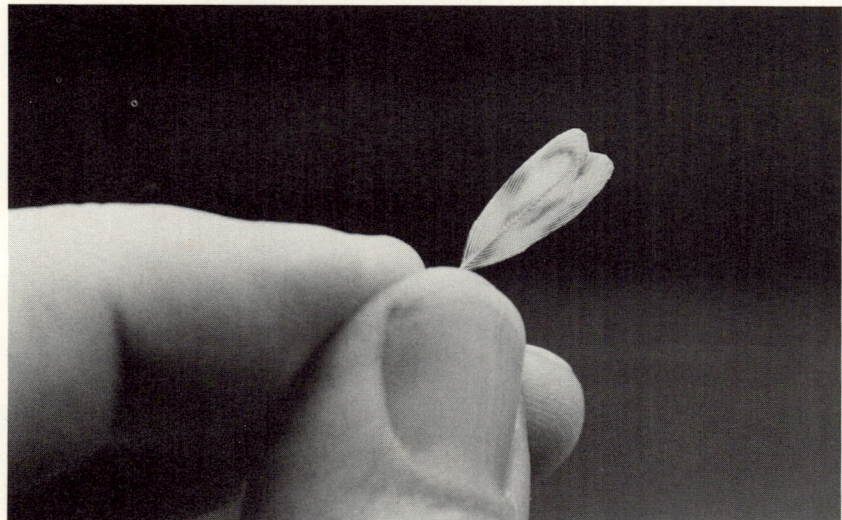

14

Apply a small drop of rubber solution to the top of the body in order to hold the wing in position.

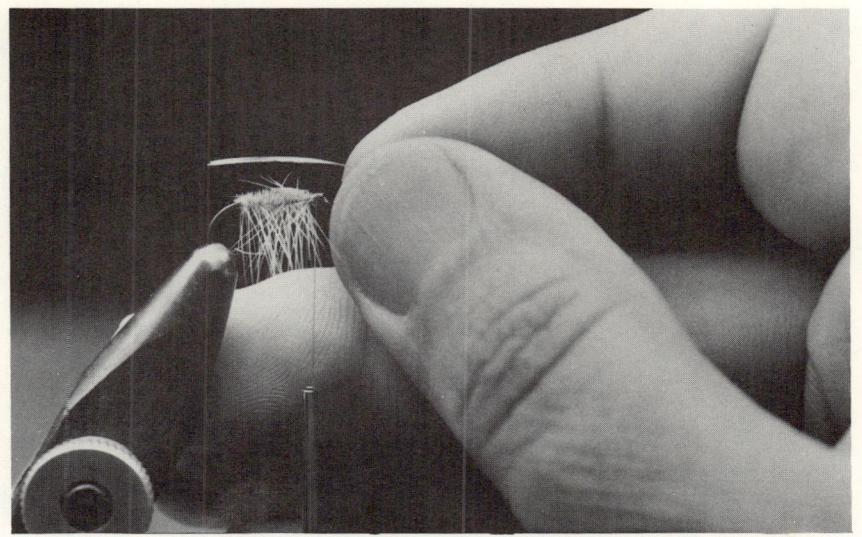

15
Place the clipped feather on top of the body so that the stem lies exactly *above* the shank of the hook.

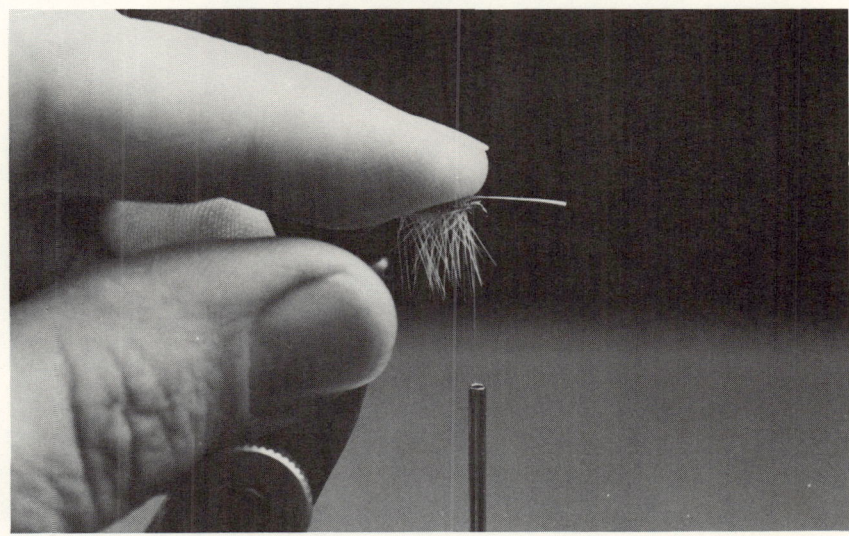

16
Hold down the feather with your forefinger for a moment. When the solution dries, the feather will be anchored to the body.

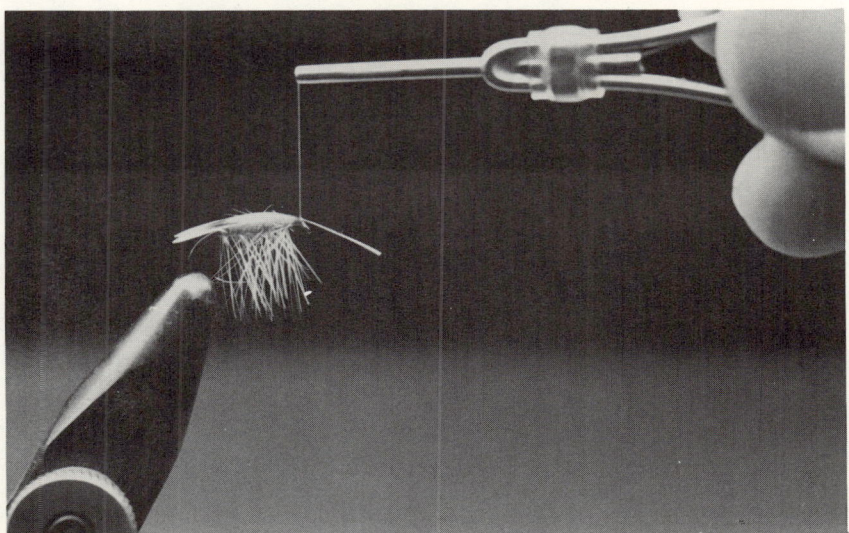

17
Beginning at the eye of the hook, wrap down the stem. The first wrap should be loose so that the stem can be positioned over the shank. Wrap five to six turns of thread to the wing and finish off the head. Lacquer the head.

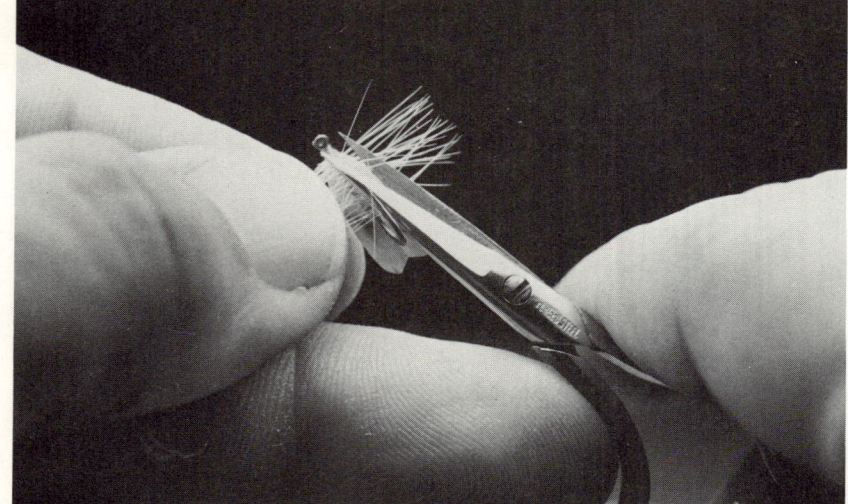

18
Remove the fly from the vise and holding it upside down, clip the hackle barbs off the bottom.

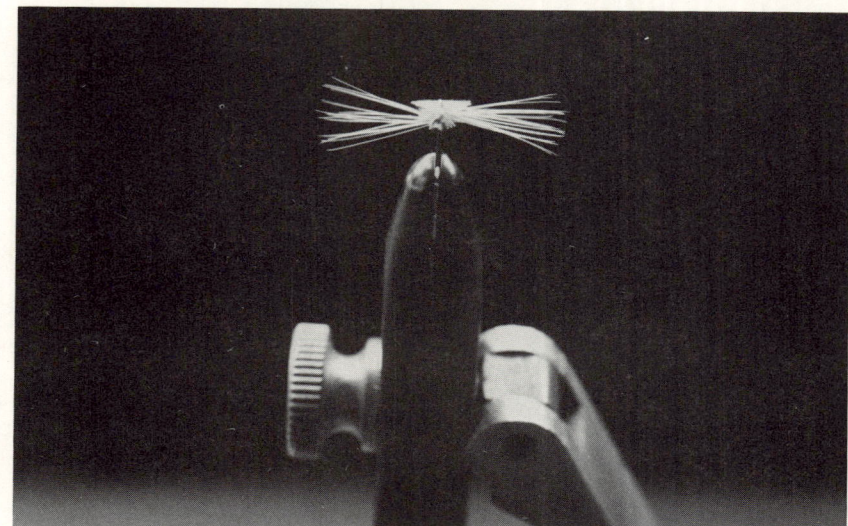

19
The hackle should lie in a horizontal plane so that the finished fly will float flush on the surface.

20
Finished flies and some of the multiplicity of bird feathers that can be used for wings. It is important to coat the feathers with a thin rubber solution.

The Adult Stone Fly
By TED NIEMEYER
Photographs by John Merwin

The ungainly, often turbulent Madison River of Montana beckoned me one spring to experience the frenzy that has come to be called the "Salmon Fly Hatch." Fly fishermen East to West share a unique excitement when the word is out that the huge stone flies are airborne. I had heard of this madness for many years, but had remained on my beloved trout and steelhead waters of Washington and British Columbia. I did succumb finally and experienced it firsthand.

The first encounter with *Pteronarcys californica* can be an exasperating experience, leaving the experienced fly fisherman lamenting a long series of failures over large fish. This is merely the initiation price we all must pay. Frustration forces each fisherman who challenges the "hatch" to try and solve the pattern/presentation riddle, and ultimately a fair share of bragging fish can be outwitted.

Fly patterns conceived to fool trout during the stone fly emergence have one common feature—they are large. Prior to my first visit to the Madison I researched patterns known to be successful, such as the Sofa Pillow, Bird's Stonefly, Nature Flies, Bi-Fly, Grizzly and Black Wulffs, Mossback, and others. All of these worked for me. Being of an inquisitive and challenging temperament, however, I sought to add my own pattern to the long list. Mine was to be more of an exact imitation than the others, and it has turned out that way.

Fishing with a bulky fly such as the Adult Stone Fly presents the uninitiated with problems not normally associated with dry-fly fishing for trout. The casting technique is more akin to bass bugging, but I abhor the rods and lines used in that kind of fishing when I'm working over trout. My casting may not be picture-book perfect and my presentation would make Kreh cry, but it gets the job done. I have a simple rule: Use whatever floating gear you like best, only change the leader to a maximum of 9 feet with a stiff butt of 90 to 99% of the diameter of the point on your fly line. My leader point has never been smaller than 3X that I can recall.

You can save the delicate presentations for better times and other trouting conditions. A good "smack" on the water with this imitation where a trout has broken water will most times bring a response. Keep the fly constantly on the water, moving it from shoreline to shoreline and all likely points in between. While it's on the water, I often give the fly added sharp twitches and try to cause a sizable commotion. Not at all in keeping with standard tactics, but a trout will move surprising distances to take a good-sized meal and this added motion may gain his attention. Your fine work at the tying bench should do the rest.

MATERIALS

HOOK: Mustad #79580, sizes 4 and 6

THREAD: black silk size 6/0 (or 4/0 or 5/0 — a matter of preference)

TAILS: two porcupine quills, small and of a brownish color, or brown-dyed Canada goose flight quills (the short, stiff side of the flight feather works best)

ABDOMEN: brownish deer body hair, or elk or antelope hair (for lighter coloration)

THORAX: turkey marabou (down), with bands of hot orange seal dubbing at specific positions

LEGS: dyed dark-brown turkey primary-flight quills, or flattened porcupine hair and dyed brown Canada goose primary-flight quills

WINGS: a matched pair of starling flight quills (select small birds)

THORAX SHELL: black duck breast feather, varnished and trimmed to shape; head: dark brown turkey marabou; eyes: porcupine hairs, knotted, clipped, and dipped in Valspar varnish

HEAD CASE: black duck breast feather, varnished and trimmed to shape

ANTENNAE: porcupine hairs

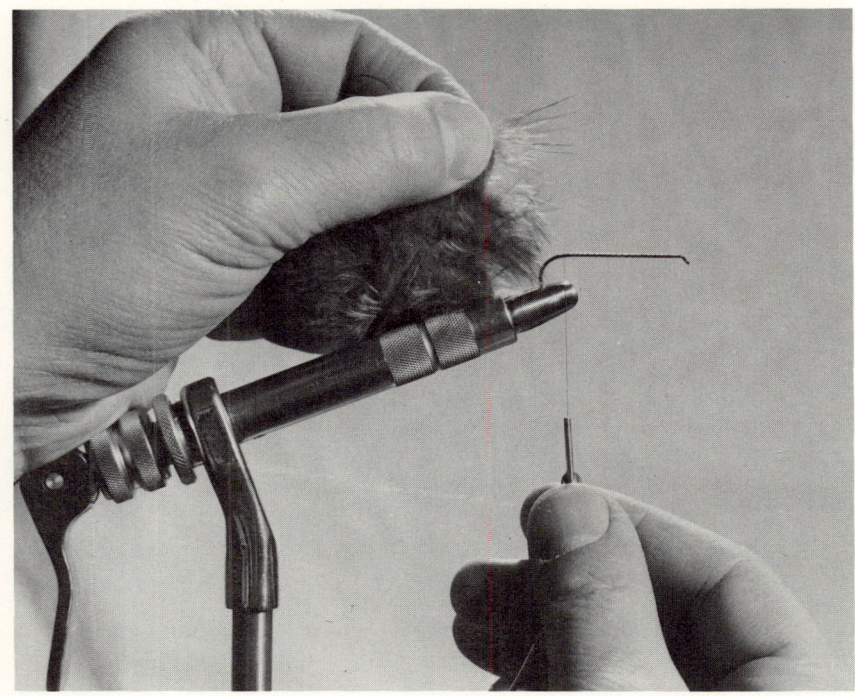

1
Having completed a single layer of tying thread on the hook shank, select a portion of turkey marabou suitable for dubbing.

2

Dub a small quantity of turkey marabou on the tying thread and form a supporting ball at the hook bend. The ball of dubbing will help spread and elevate the tails.

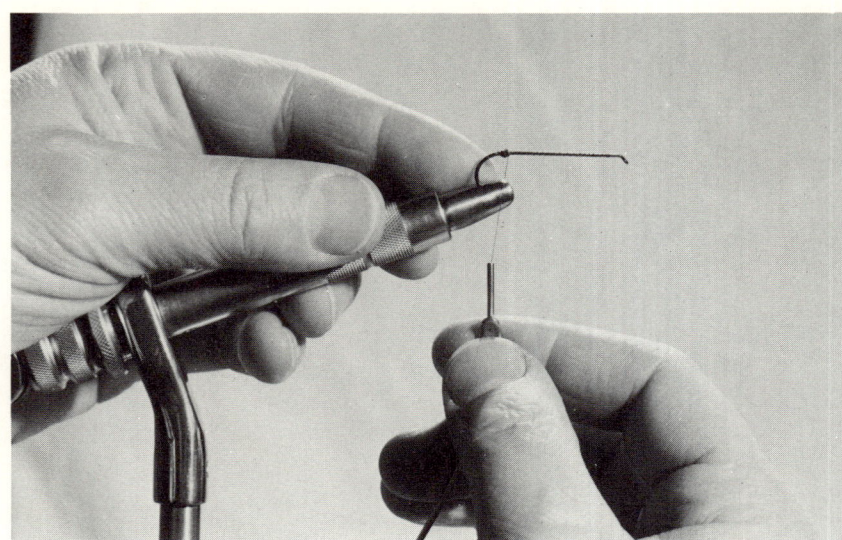

3

Select suitable porcupine quills for tails. Pay particular attention to color and shape when matching them.

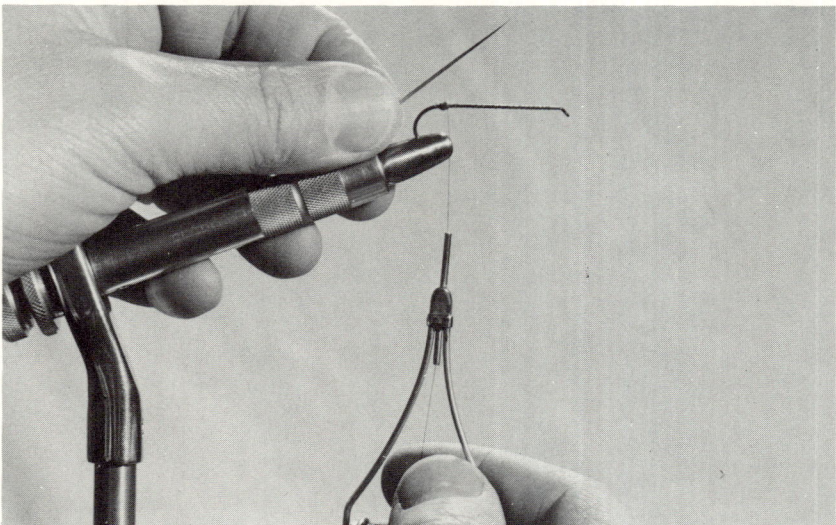

4

Making sure they are of equal length, secure the two tails in a slightly elevated V. Tie the tails firmly in place with figure-8 turns of thread around their base.

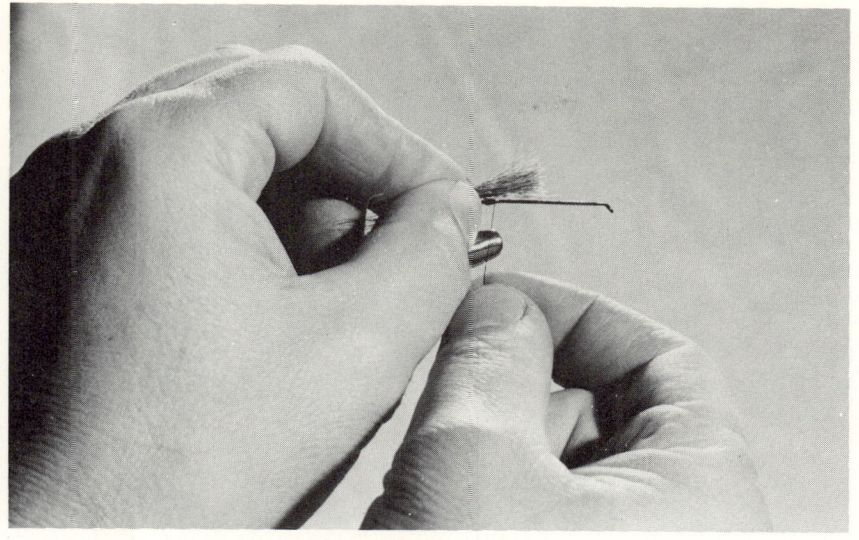

5

Select a good floating quality deer-body hair and commence spinning small quantities from tail to eye. Fill the hook shank to a point at least two-thirds of the total distance from hook bend to hook eye.

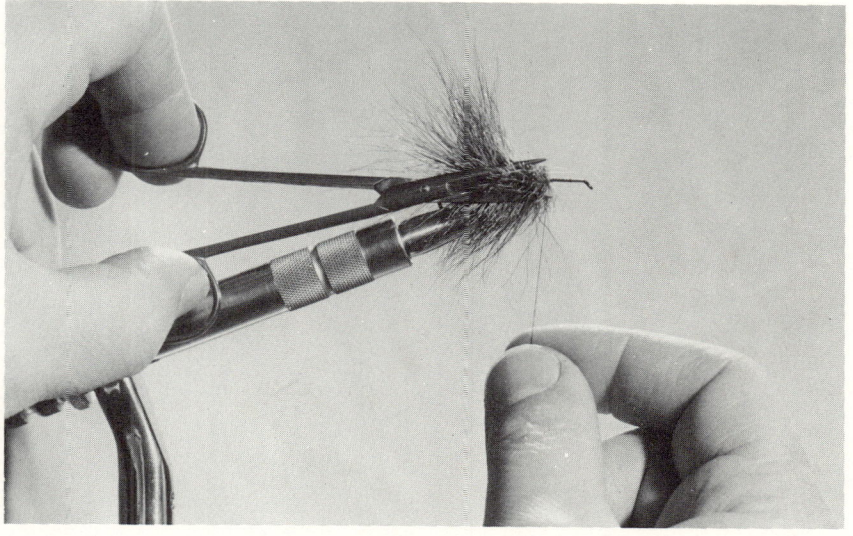

6

Trim the spun deer hair to a flat oval shape. The body form should be flatter on top and cut quite close to the hook shank as it approaches the thorax area.

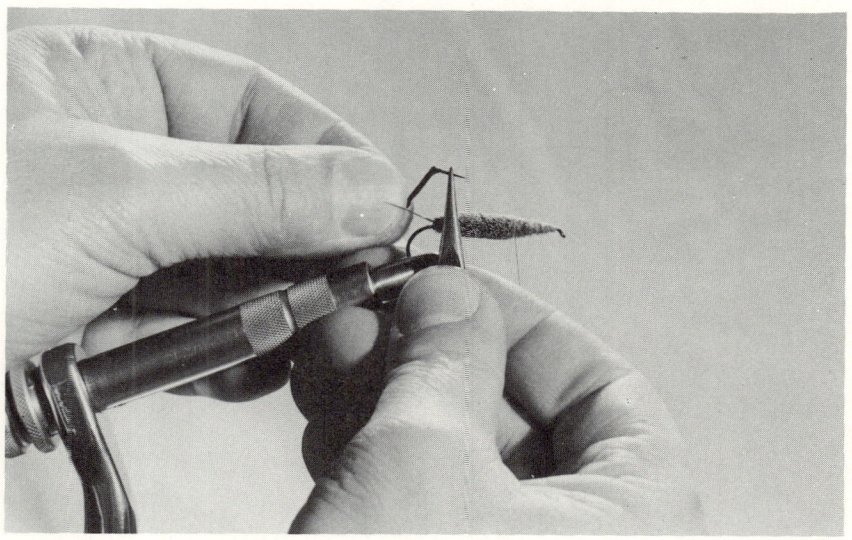

7

Select and match six porcupine quills and flatten each quill by drawing it between thumbnail and forefinger. Grasp the quill with tweezers, form a loop, and complete a simple knot. Fine-pointed tweezers are essential for this procedure.

8

To secure each leg, place the butt diagonally across the hook shank and figure-8 the tying thread over the butt of the quill several times. Bend the excess of the quill butt parallel to the hook shank and bind it down. This will lock each leg in place. Complete the tying in of the first four legs (rear and middle pairs).

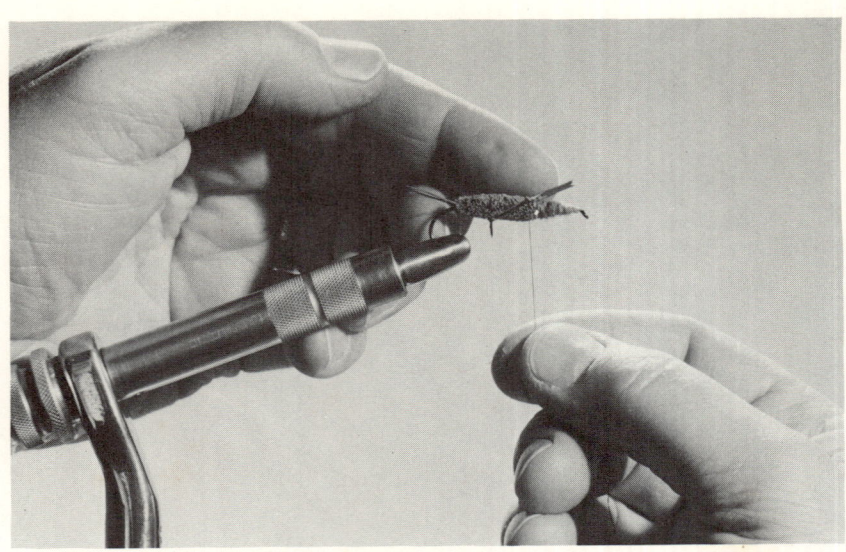

9

For the antennae, select two long, thin porcupine hairs, placing one on each side of the hook shank. The tips should extend well beyond the hook eye. Bind the hairs firmly, pull on the butt ends, and position the hairs for proper length.

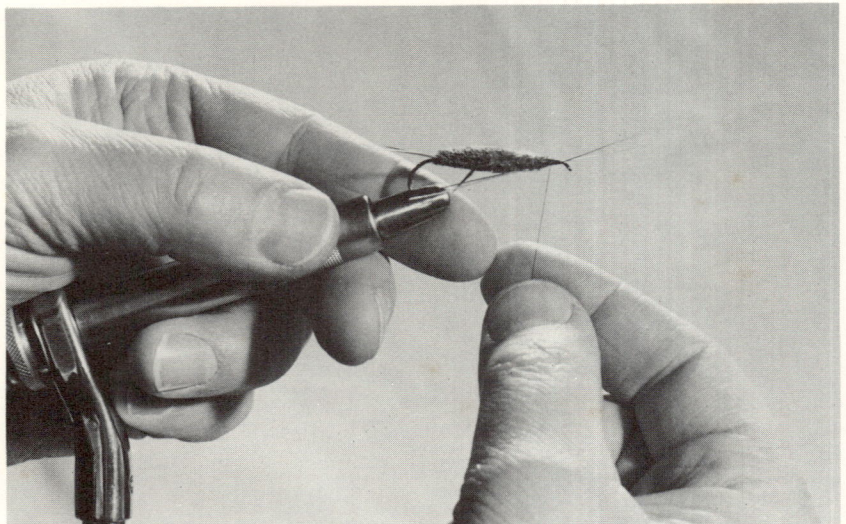

10

Select two matching starling flight quills, right and left. Trim the base of each feather to eliminate bulky excess material. Dub a generous quantity of turkey marabou over the thorax area. Do not allow this area to become lumpy.

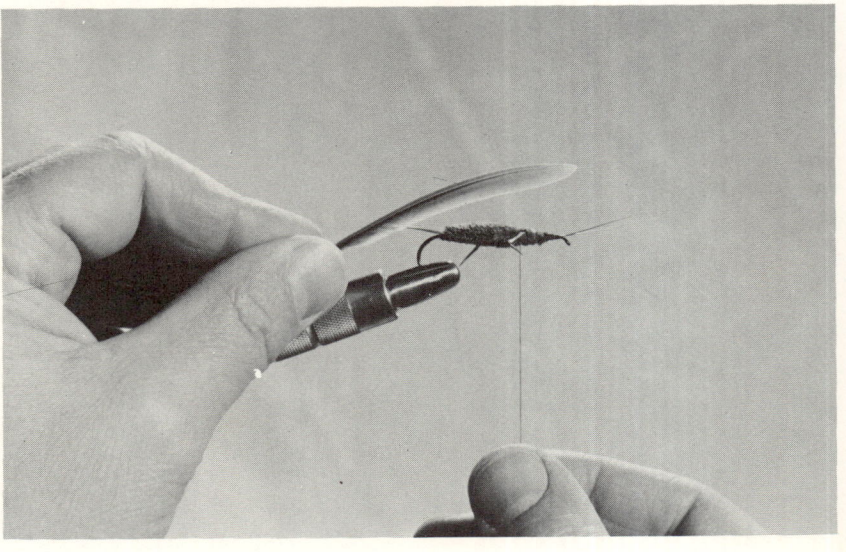

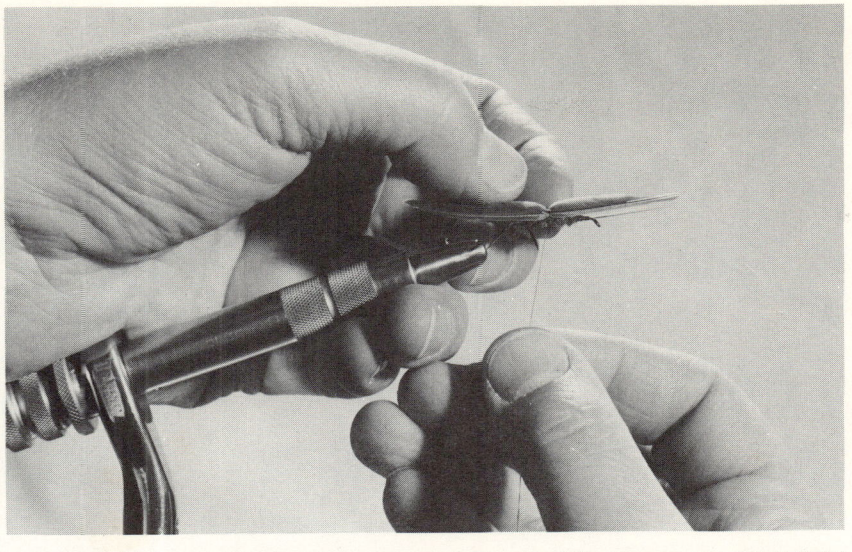

11

Lay the wings over the abdomen one at a time and bind tightly with the tying thread. The pair should lie flat (not tent style) and extend slightly longer than the tails.

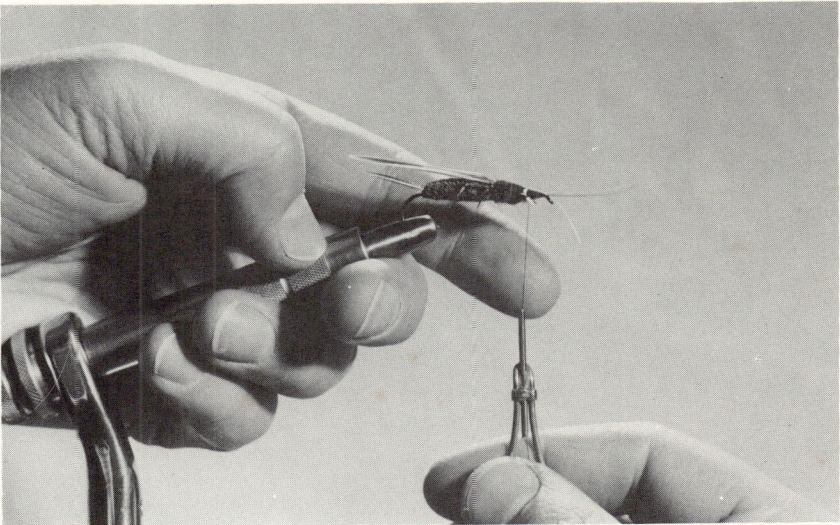

12

Move the tying thread toward the hook eye and bind in the final set of legs. Duplicate the method stated for the first two sets. The position of the front legs is about 1/8 inch behind the eye of the hook.

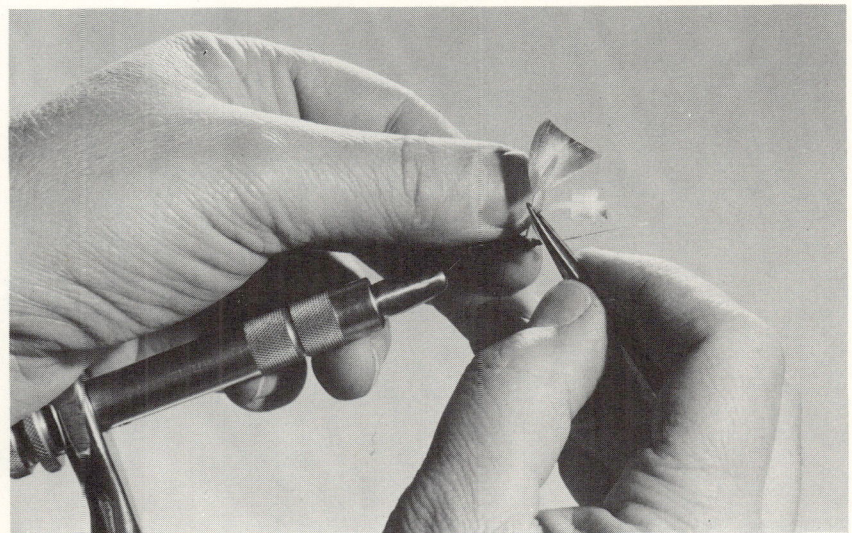

13

Select a black duck breast feather. Apply a thin coat of varnish and allow to dry (I usually prepare these well in advance to avoid delay on the day I am tying). Trim the feather to a small rectangular shape, leaving a small tip of stem on each end for ease in securing the feather in place.

14

Dub a small amount of hot orange seal fur on the tying silk and proceed to secure the black duck feather (upside down, extending toward the hook bend) directly over the wing base. Bind securely.

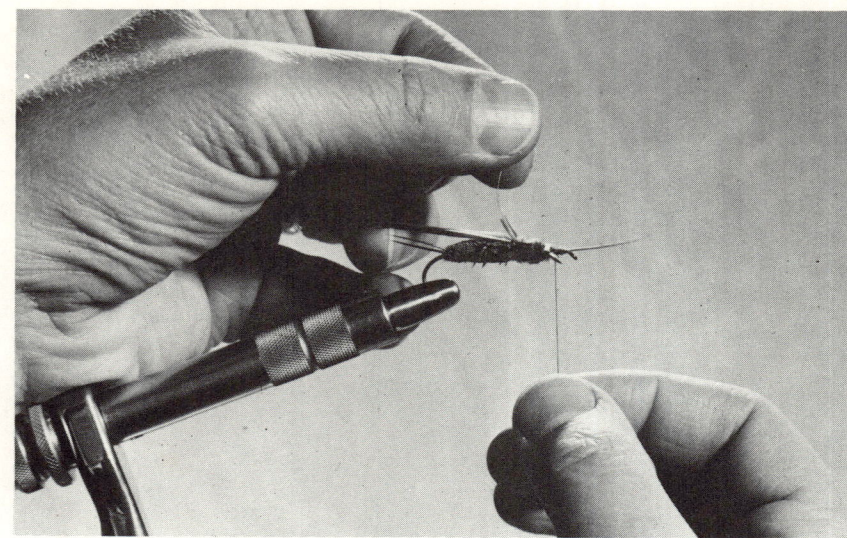

15

Apply additional turkey-down dubbing to a position just in front of the forward set of legs. Pull the black duck-feather stem forward and bind it tightly behind the forward set of legs. Bend any excess stem upright. Select a matching pair of eyes, formed from knotted and varnished porcupine hairs.

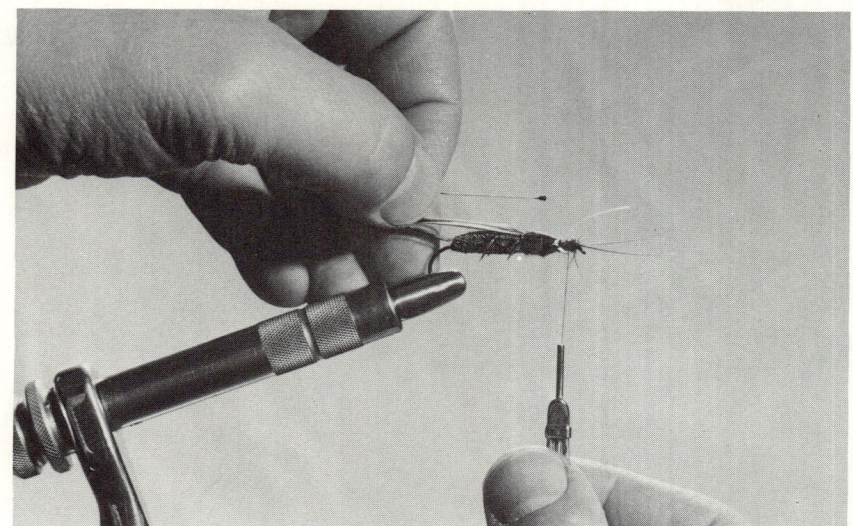

16

Place the butts of the porcupine hairs, with eyes extended, across the hook shank and bind with figure-8 turns of tying thread. Pull on the hair butts to position the eyes close to the head. Bend the butts of hair parallel to the hook shank and bind firmly.

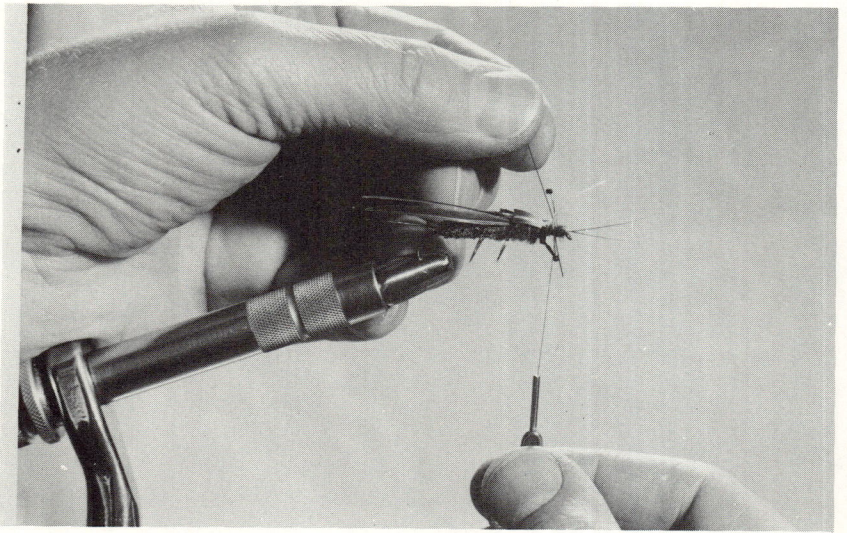

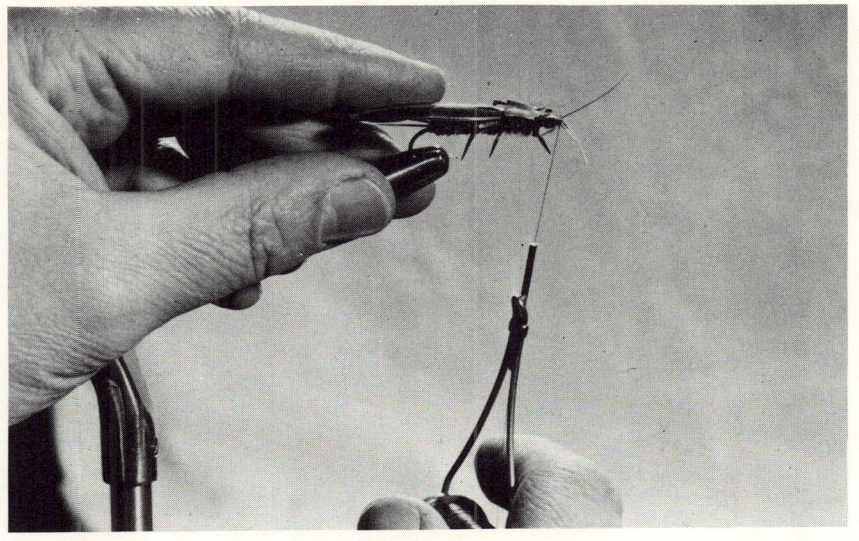

17
Dub a small quantity of turkey marabou in and about the eyes, forming a full head. Pull the stem of black duck feather down and bind firmly. It is necessary to whip a large head. Three or four turns of the finishing knot are sufficient.

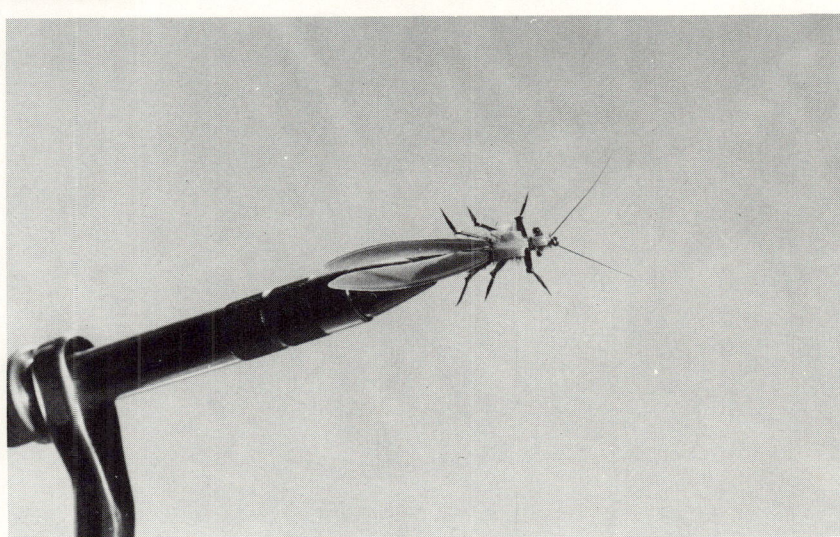

18
The overall appearance of the finished fly should be fat and juicy. A top and bottom profile are more important than the side profile.

The Hair-Wing Matuka
By ERIC W. PEPER
Photographs by Bob Linsenman

My introduction to the Matuka pattern came through Joe Bates's book *Streamer Fly Tying and Fishing*, where it is called the "Matuku." Bates cites Australia, New Zealand, and England as the countries where the fly was then (1950) in use. Since that time, the pattern has become quite popular in the United States, thanks to such anglers as Dave Whitlock, Doug Swisher, and Carl Richards. The original Matuka pattern calls for a wing and tail made from hackle feathers, with the hackle stems laced to the body by a separate thread or by the ribbing material. A hackle collar in front of the wing may be used. Normally, four hackle feathers are used for the wing.

    I began tying and using the Matuka several years ago and was impressed with its effectiveness on trout, bass, and other species. Several features of the pattern bothered me, however. If great care is not used when the fly is put away after use, the wing becomes bent (if wet) and the pattern's performance is impaired on the next use. The hackle feathers were not as durable as I would have liked, and I wanted a pattern that had a "meatier" appearance in the water. The solution was to duplicate the Matuka's conformation using hair fibers. My first attempts utilized deer hair for wing, tail, and "spikes" (those wings positioned midway on the body). These patterns rode high in the water due to the buoyancy of the deer hair. Later attempts used polar bear hair throughout, and the solid hair gave the sinking characteristic that was sought.

Now I tie the Hair-Wing Matuka using a variety of materials which provide the variety of features needed, so that the pattern fishes at the proper depth as a function of the materials rather than of added weight. The illustrations show the Matuka being tied with bucktail for wing and tail, and fox squirrel for the spikes. The chenille body may be replaced with dubbed fur, yarn, or other material. The color is the choice of the tyer, and minnow imitations may be achieved using either dyed or natural materials. I fish the pattern more as an attractor, so I let my own creativity dictate the combinations.

My experience has been that the Hair-Wing is more effective than the original pattern, primarily I suspect because of its bulkier appearance in the water and the more natural shape obtained through a flared, rather than pointed tail. By using hair I have gained the convenience features of durability and packability that I sought, while the variety of hair available lets me create a fly that fishes deep or shallow without having to add lead. The Hair-Wing Matuka is relatively easy to tie. The hackle collar is optional, but helps to achieve the natural shape. Whip one up and take a look at it in the water. I think you will see what I mean.

MATERIALS
HOOK: #9575, size 4 (optional)
THREAD: black
TAIL: bucktail
BODY: black chenille, with deer hair spike
WING: bucktail
COLLAR: saddle hackle

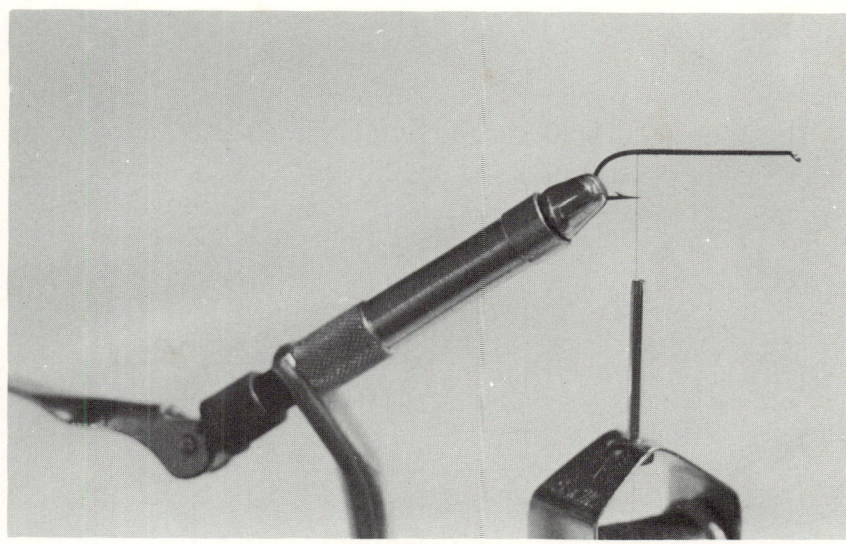

1
Begin by wrapping the tying thread the length of the hook to provide a nonslip base for the bucktail.

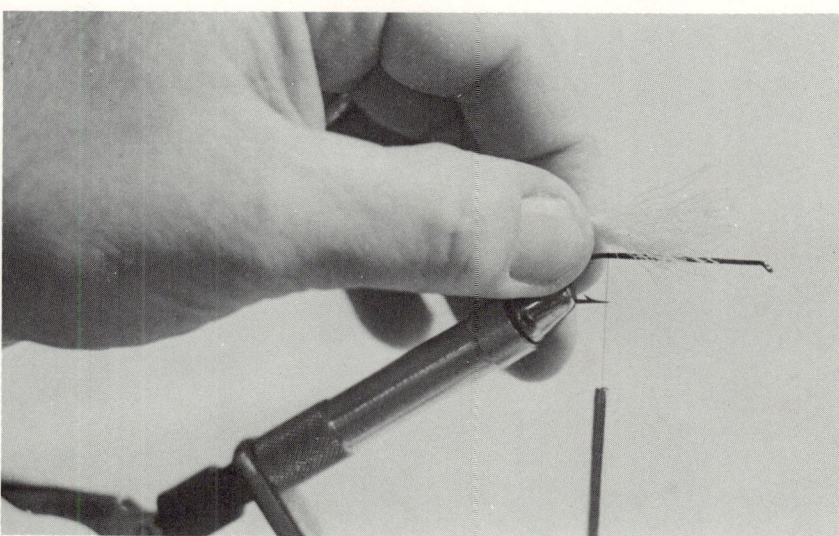

2
Measure the bucktail so that the fly's tail will be as long as the hook shank and the butts extend to the tip of the loop on the loop eye.

87

3

Tie the tail on so that the bucktail fibers are on top of the hook, above the point, but surround the hook as they are tied forward.

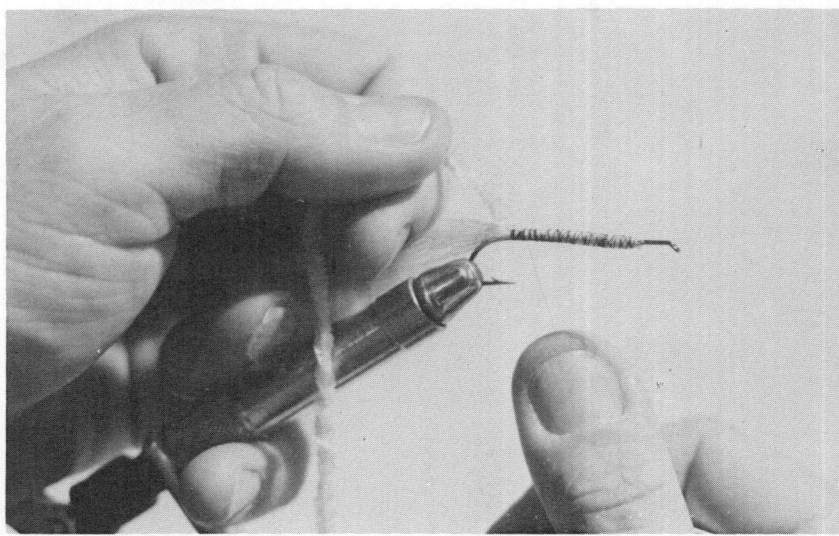

4

Tie in a strand of chenille at the initial tail wraps, and make two turns to start the body.

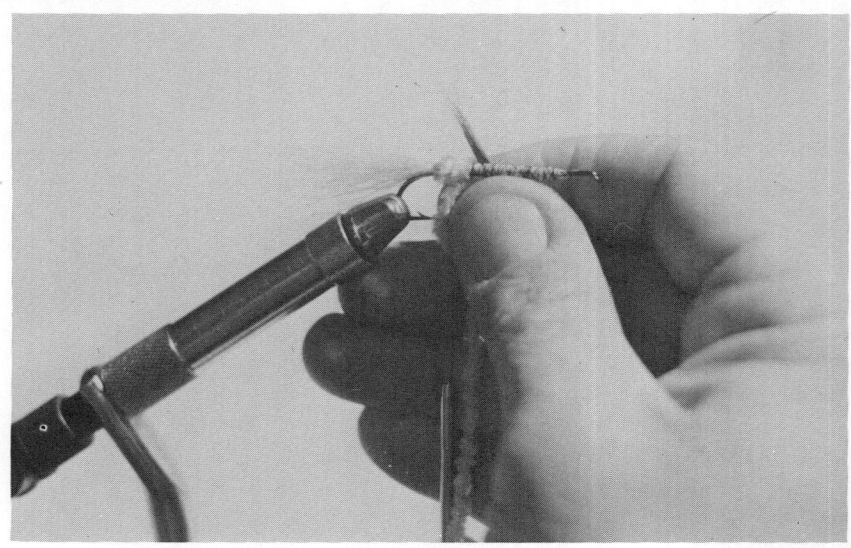

5

The first spike, or wing, should be a little longer than the gape of the hook.

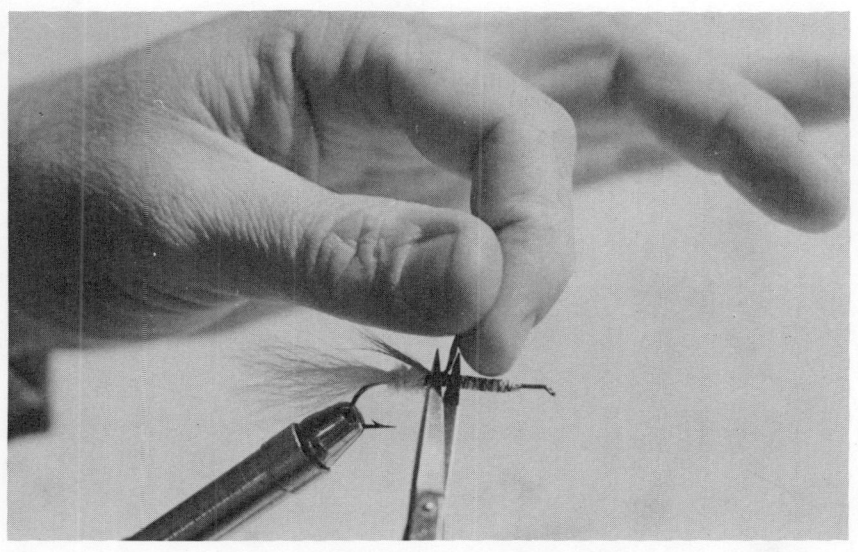

6
Tie in the spike and clip the butts of the hair approximately two chenille wraps forward.

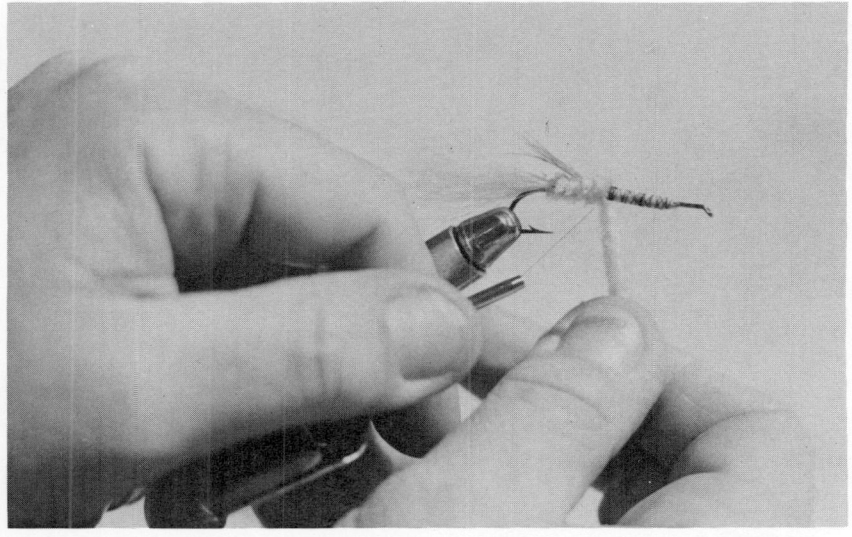

7
Make two wraps of chenille; tie in a second, slightly longer spike; and repeat with two more chenille wraps and a third spike, longer yet.

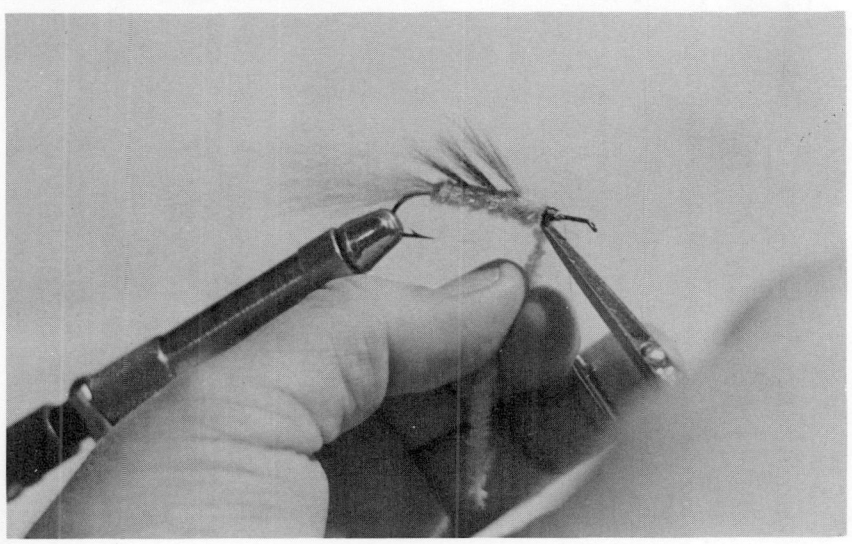

8
Make two wraps of chenille in front of the third spike and tie off. The scissors are shown to accent the length of "working" hook remaining for wing and hackle.

9

Tie on a bucktail wing that is the length of the hook and add two turns of chenille over the wing wraps.

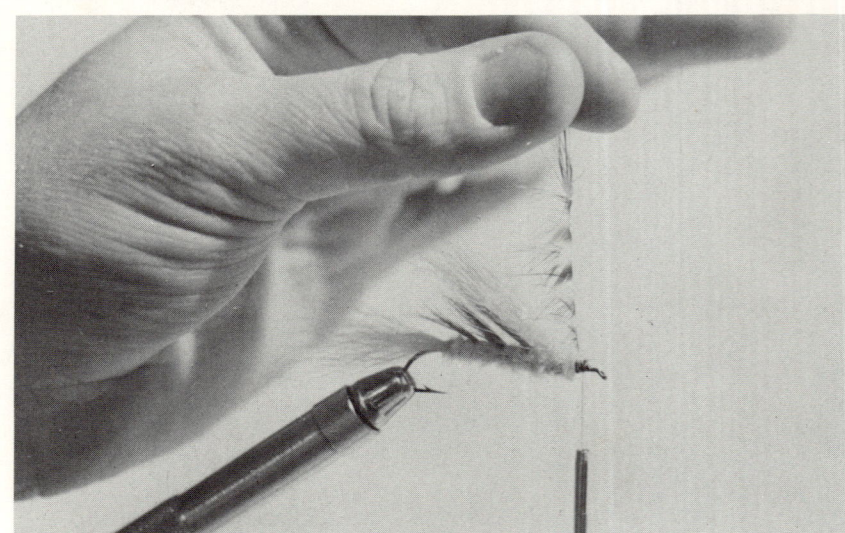

10

Tie in a hen hackle by the tip and fold back the fibers.

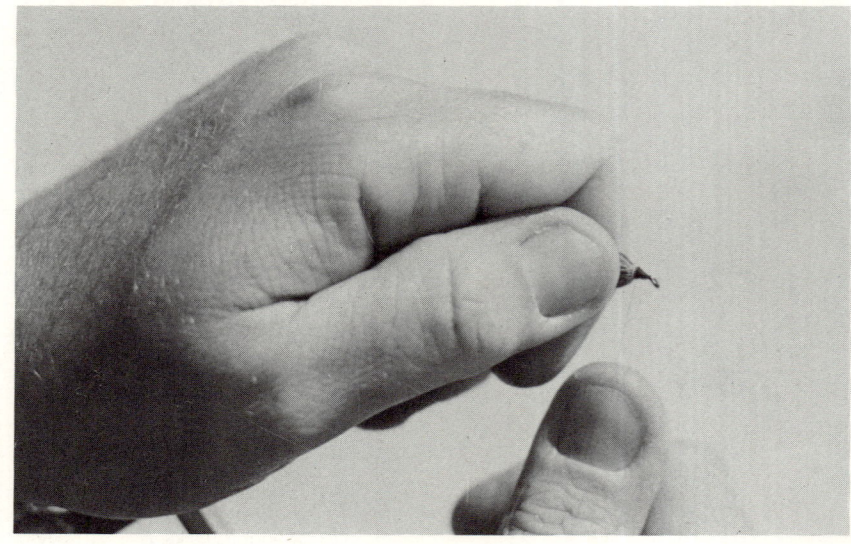

11

After wrapping and tying off the hackle, stroke the fibers to the rear and form a neat, tapered head.

12
After whip-finishing and lacquering, your fly should look like this.

Vinny's Midge
By JOHN SHOLLENBERGER
Photographs by Irv Swope

Early last May I spent a day fishing at Henryville with a good friend, Dr. Vincent Ringrose. On that day the only significant hatch was a large black midge, a true Diptera. My host, who especially enjoys midge-fishing, was very frustrated by the numbers of rejections we were receiving with our imitations. The conventional black midge patterns, with or without wings or tails, all seemed to be only fair representations at best in the eyes of the selectively sipping browns, especially in the slower runs and flats.

Two days later my friend drove down to my home to fish with me on Clark's Creek, and he brought with him suggestions for two black midge patterns. He had designed them while carefully observing the numerous live midges on and around the lamp in his motel room back at Henryville. One pattern represented a resting midge, the other the same midge in a spent position. I tied both in sizes 20, 22, 24, and 28.

Subsequent testing by Vinny and myself on several streams showed the resting pattern to be vastly superior, so much so that Vinny claims it to be a "fish on every cast" fly, provided the tippet is fine enough (7x or 8x) and the placement is accurate, since a midging fish rarely moves more than an inch or two for its prey. There are several features we feel to be important: Prominent antennae; a long, slender, nontapered abdomen with only faintly visible segments; a slightly delta-shaped configuration of the whitish-grey wings; sparse black hackle for the legs; and no tails. The best hook size is 22, although an 18 was used in the photographs to provide more detail.

MATERIALS
HOOK: Mustad #94840, size 22
THREAD: 8–0 black silk
BODY: peacock quill
WING: light-blue dun
HACKLE: black
ANTENNAE: black

1
Start your thread two or three wraps behind the eye, and continue it back to the place on the bend so that when you let the bobbin hang free, the thread will be even with the back of the barb.

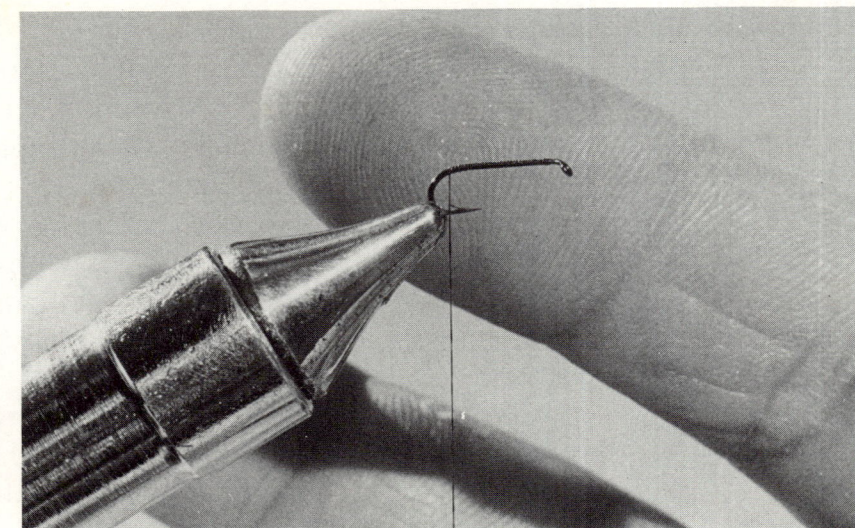

2
Select a peacock quill from below the eye. Quills from this part of the feather do not have the sharp dark edge of those taken from the eye of the feather.

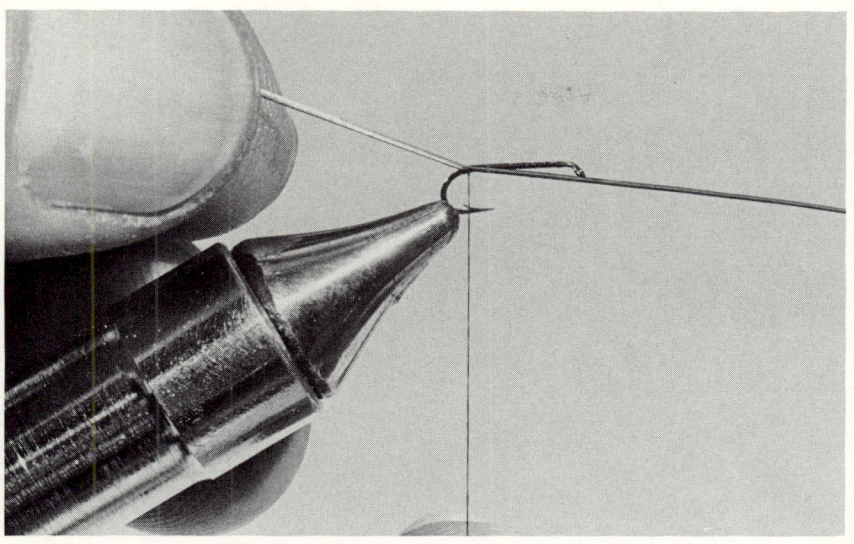

3
Strip off the herl and tie the quill to the shank of the hook.

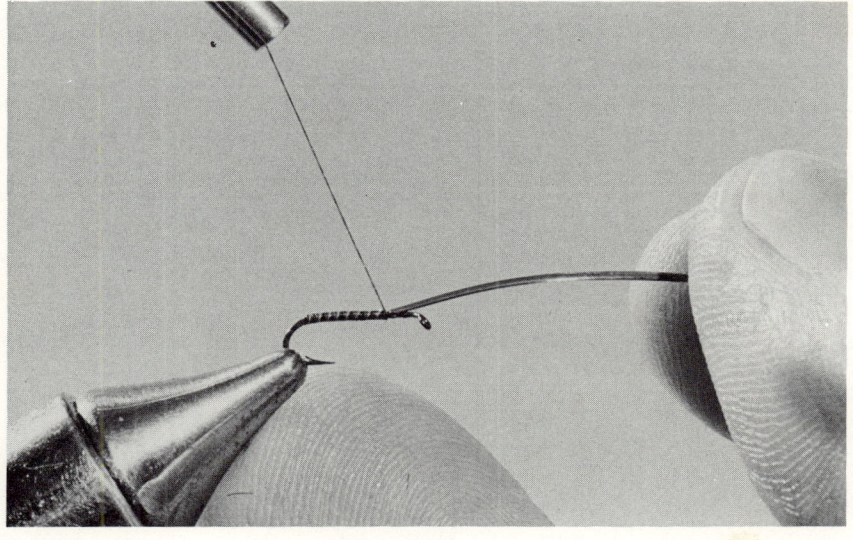

4
Wind the thread up three-quarters of the way to the eye of the hook. Do not build up a body with thread. Keep wraps uniform to maintain a slim appearance. Then wind the quill to same point.

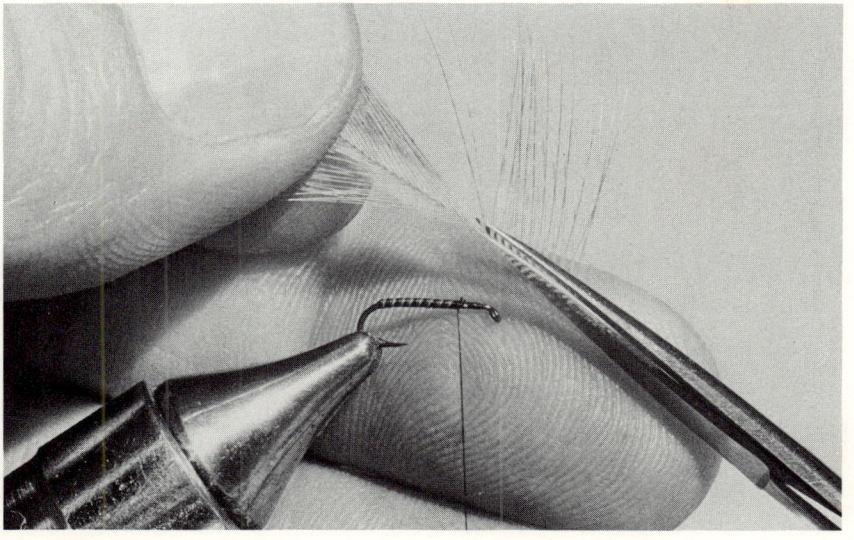

5
Select two light-blue dun feathers with fairly long fibers for the wing. Place together, both face side up, then trim off fibers halfway up the stem.

6

With thumb and forefinger, pull a small group of fibers in the opposite direction, keeping a tight grip on the fibers at all times.

7

Tie the wings directly on top of the hook shank with three or four wraps of the thread.

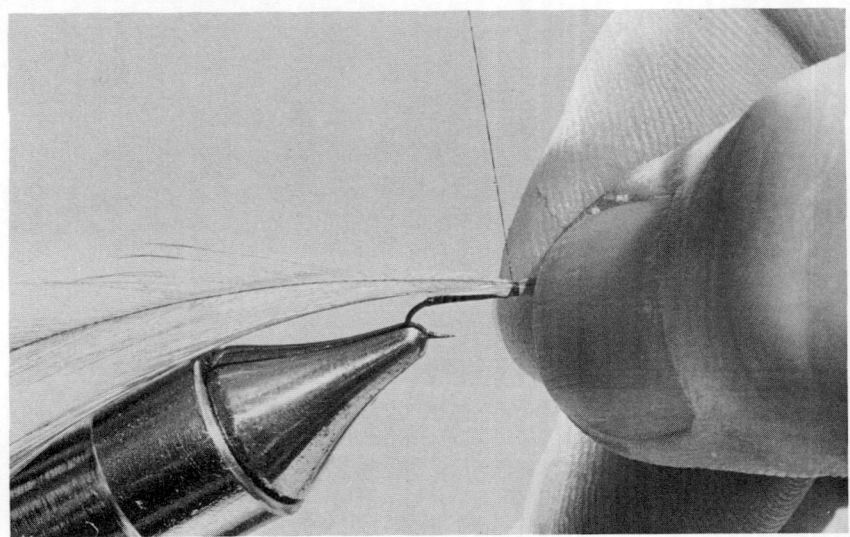

8

Figure-8 the thread two or three times between the wings to get a slightly delta-shaped configuration.

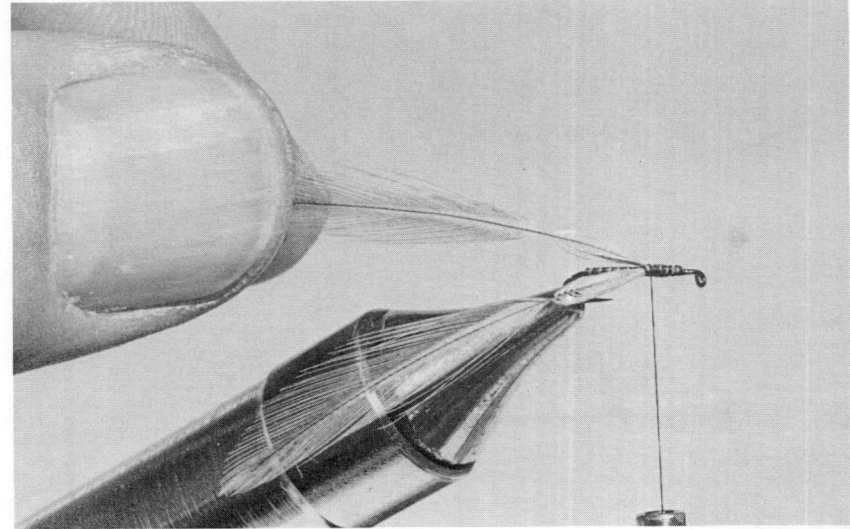

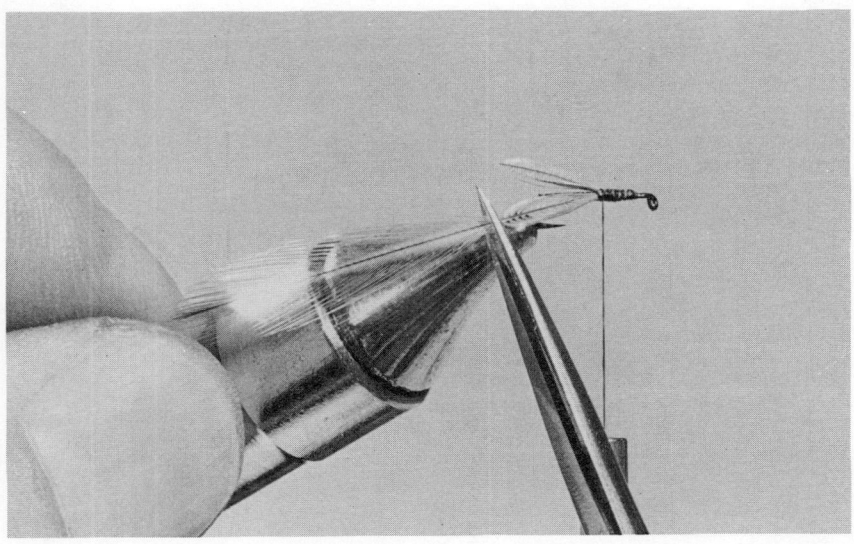

9

Trim off the tips of the feathers next to the fibers in the reversed position.

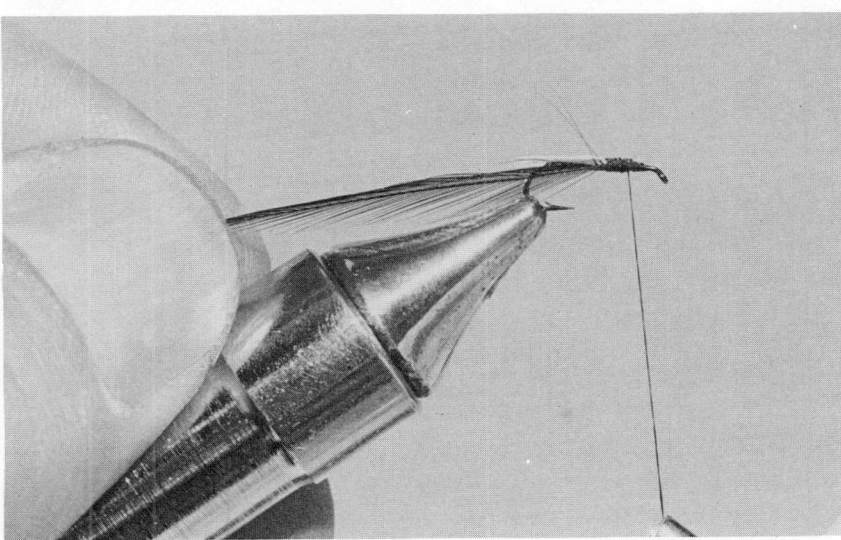

10

Select one black hackle, a size larger than you would normally use (the legs are rather long on the real fly). Trim away the web and tie it on the side of the shank with the face side of the feather toward you.

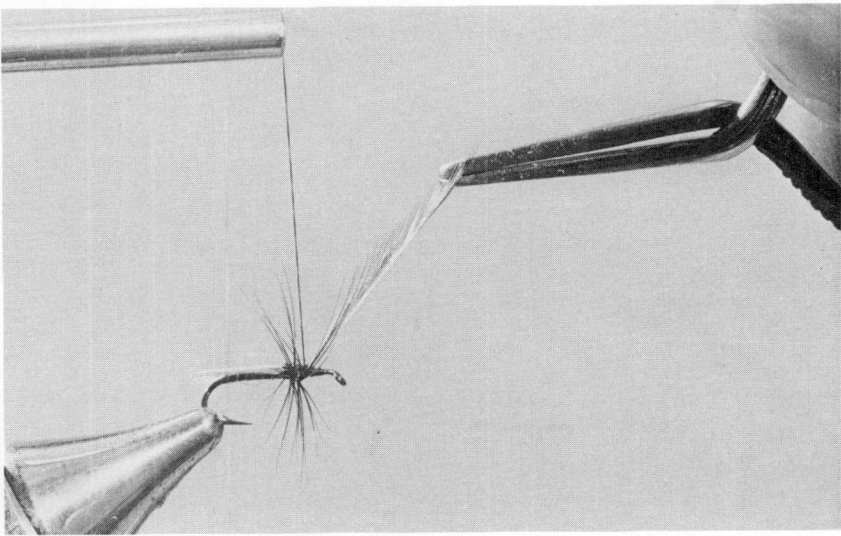

11

Keep the hackle sparse, make only one or two wraps with the feather, and then tie off.

12

For the antennae, select two small black feathers. Trim away the fibers next to the stem.

13

Tie in the antennae at the head so that the contour of the quill turns away from the eye of the hook. Trim to length.

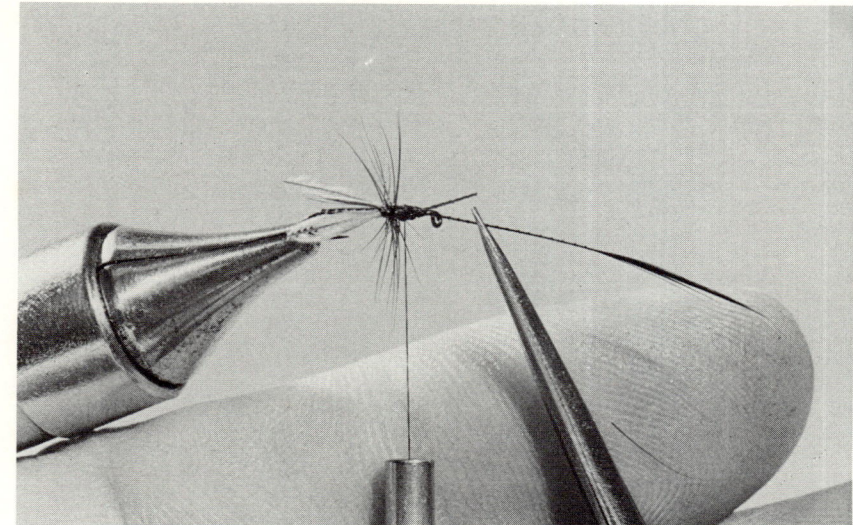

14

Lift up the antennae, half-hitch, then whip-finish.

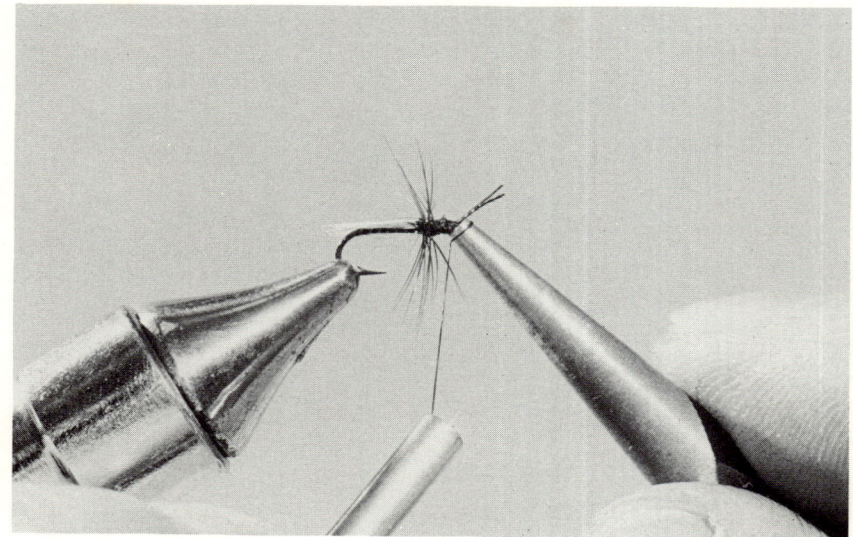

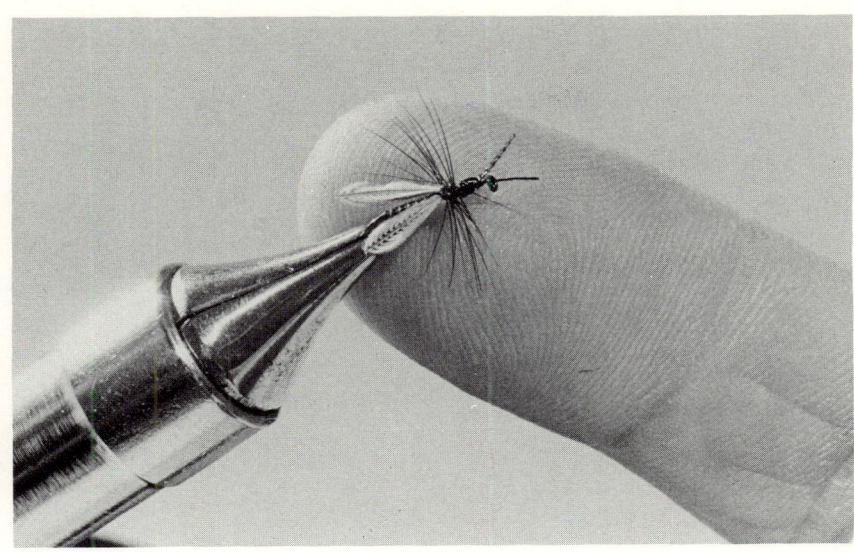

15
The finished fly.

The Cardinelle
By DICK SURETTE
Photographs by Andrew Wainwright

Some of the most popular fishing flies in northern New England for the past seventy-five years have been the streamer/bucktail types, a basic fly for early season angling. Around the turn of the century, Herb Welch of Oquoussoc, Maine, first tied his Black Ghost, Welch Rabbit, and Jane Craig patterns. Other tyers such as Joe Stickney, with his Warden's Worry, and Carrie Stevens, with her Gray Ghost and Wizard, set the tone for the flies to follow. Since that time, new colors, materials, and theories have come along but the basic design and format of the bucktails and streamers has changed very little.

During April and May, the smelt move out of the lakes and up into the rivers to spawn. They come in hordes, with the salmon right behind them. Frequently, the run of smelt is nocturnal and the spawning smelt run back to the protective deep lake during the early hours of dawn, so some of the best fishing is at dawn. This angling requires patience: a river may be devoid of fish one day and loaded the next.

The other use of streamers and bucktail is for trolling on lakes and ponds right after ice-out. In Maine, New Hampshire, and Vermont the ice disappears the third week in April, on an average, and a week or two later in the extreme northern areas. About two weeks after ice-out, trolling for landlocks, lakers, and a few odd brown trout begins in earnest. The basic trolling patterns are the Gray Ghost, Green Ghost, Nine Three, Barnes Special, Red

Gray Ghost, Winnipesaukee Smelt, Blue Smelt, and Mickey Finn. Tandem models of these flies can use size 2 to 4 front hooks and 4 to 6 rear hooks. The rear hook can ride up or down; sometimes a small double or treble hook is used for the rear.

The Cardinelle is opposite in basic design to the aforementioned patterns. This fly was first tied by Bill Chiba of Springfield, Mass., in the late 1960s. Bill showed the fly to Paul Kukonen of Worcester, Mass., who made a few minor revisions. The Cardinelle has taken all species of trout, Atlantic salmon, small and large mouth bass, walleyed pike, northern pike, striped bass, and coho salmon along with other saltwater species over the past few years. The bright colors of the fly place it in the attractor class, and fish usually take it with vigor.

The materials for the Cardinelle are inexpensive and readily available. The cerise wing of marabou is distinctive and dyed especially for this fly. Its main asset is the pulsating action of the soft material as the water reacts on the wing. By using a slow retrieve, fast retrieve, or a staccato twitch in fast water, the action is always there in the fly. The Cardinelle is also easy to tie, another reason to give it a place in your fly book. Imaginative tyers can develop a series of Cardinelles by dying white marabou a variety of fluorescent colors. Try to harmonize the body and the underwing colors to balance out the overall fly design. Be sure not to make the wing too long. Fish tend to follow this fly, but may be unsure about taking it and may take a very quick swipe. If the material in the wing is too long, you will end up with a short strike.

MATERIALS
HOOK: Mustad 3665A
THREAD: hot orange
BODY: fluorescent orange wool
UNDERWING: fluorescent orange wool or nylon
WING: cerise marabou
HACKLE: yellow saddle

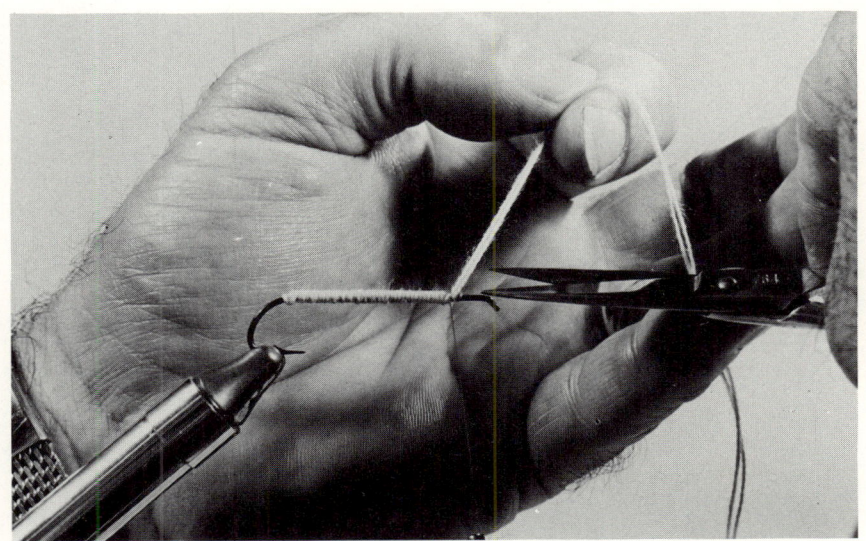

1

Wrap fluorescent wool along the entire length of the shank of the hook to make the body. Seal Ex, Spun Fur, angora, sparkle yarn, or acrylic fiber can be substituted for wool. Synthetic material can be spun on or mixed in a blender. Tease the material out with a bodkin or X-Acto blade to give the fuzzy, translucent effect. A fine, soft fur such as beaver or rabbit can be dubbed on first as a base.

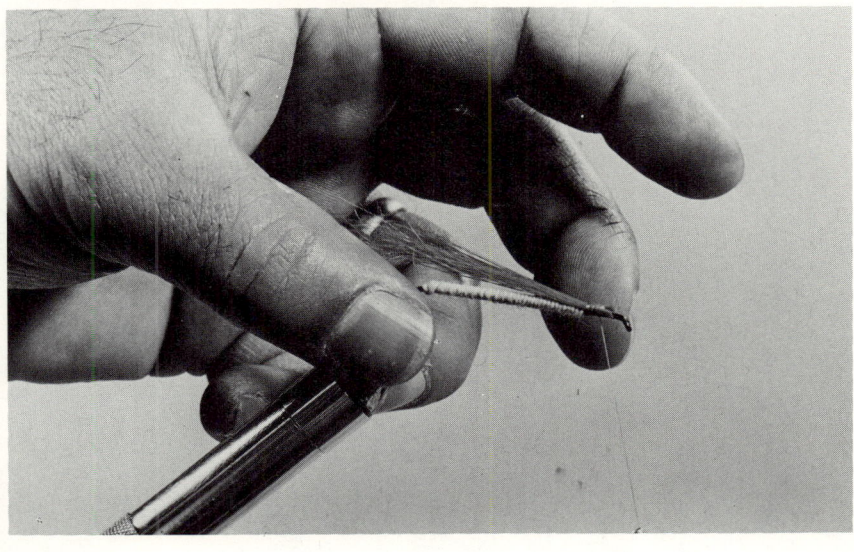

2

Attach the underwing of fluorescent orange hair or nylon, keeping it sparse. The underwing should be faint, not obvious. Despite its wild colors, the Cardinelle follows the basic color scheme of lightest color on the bottom, darker in the mid underwing, and darkest on top. This duplicates the baitfish, which often have a subtle color tone in the midpart of the body that is seen most readily by the trout.

3

Using cerise marabou, attach a good-sized bunch of wing material directly over the underwing. Remember that the marabou wing will decrease greatly when wet, so be generous. Note the length of the wing, the most colorful, and eye-catching part of the fly.
fly.

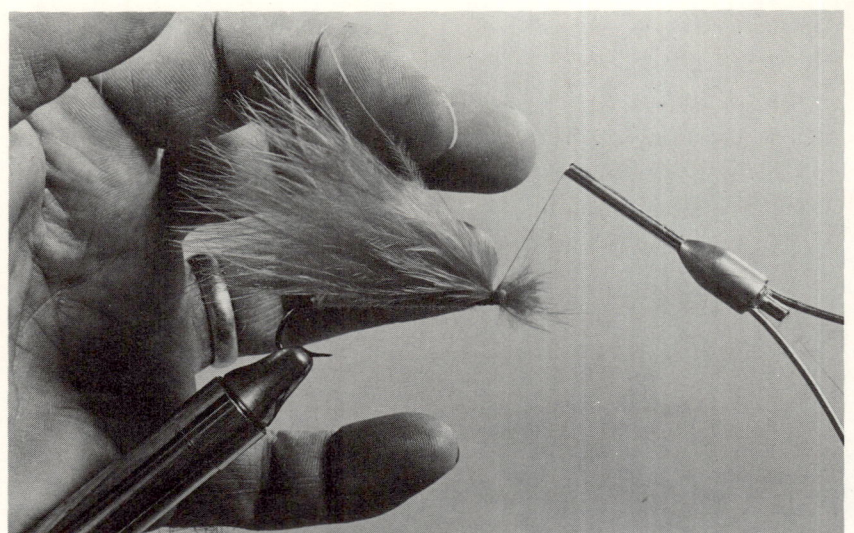

4

Place one long, soft, yellow saddle as a hackle and tie the collar on wet style. Whip-finish a fluorescent orange head. The collar adds grace and sparkle, as well as contrast. Be careful to select the right length of saddle to do the job properly. Carefully measure the head length and the space left at the end of the fly. A few turns will get the color in place, then carefully wind back to the rear of the head of the fly to pull the hackles into place and fold slightly with the fingertips to get the exact positioning of the hackles. Then proceed to complete the fly with the proper tapered head.

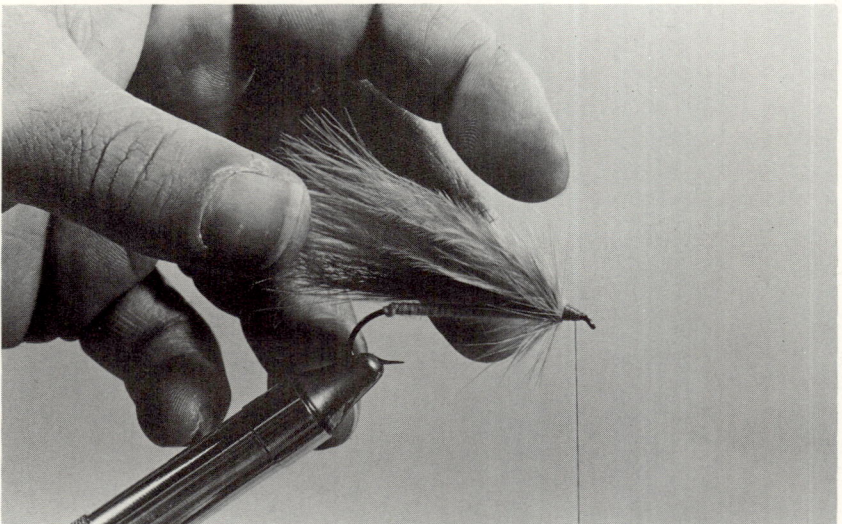

5

The completed Cardinelle.

15

The Painted Lady
By RALPH WAHL
Assisted by Dick Van Demark
Photographs by Ralph Wahl

Most West Coast steelhead anglers I know tie their own flies. They range from simple yarn affairs to elaborate combinations of tinsel, feathers, and bucktails that rival the best Atlantic salmon patterns. And because we can only speculate as to what triggers a steelhead into taking a fly, we formulate our own theories and tie patterns to justify them. If we reason that the fish retain memories of ocean feeding, we tie something that resembles shrimp. If we appeal to their predatory instinct, we offer them bright and gaudy flies and swim them seductively through the currents. And if we insist they feed while in fresh water, we offer them dark patterns and nymphlike bugs, and in low water we may go to high-riding floaters.

Our choice of pattern is highly personal and ofttimes illogical to others. The result is hundreds of various color and material combinations, all of which, at some time or another, appear to have taken steelhead. Of course the *best* pattern is the one on the end of the leader when a fish takes. Thus are favorites made.

For some thirty-five years, through continual evolution, Painted Lady has become mine. It is not only a taking pattern but a flashing jewel in my fly box. Its half-painted, half-tinseled body is different from most conventional attractor patterns. And the fluorescent red stripe and painted eye set it apart from all others.

MATERIALS

HOOK: Mustad Limerick, #36890 sizes 4 and 2
TAIL: section from goose primary, hot orange
BODY: wide silver tinsel, upper half painted fluorescent yellow, red fluorescent stripe full length of body
WING: bucktail, red fluorescent over yellow
HEAD: built up with black tying thread
EYE: painted black pupil on white

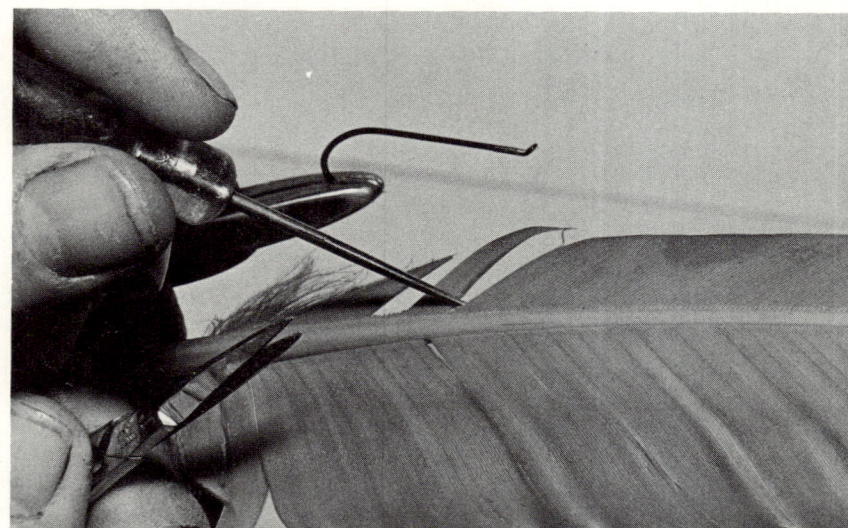

1
Prepare the tail by cutting a section 1/16 inch wide, ¾ inch long from dyed orange goose primary. To keep the feather from splitting, spray the shiny side along the quill with Grumbacher Tuffilm spray.

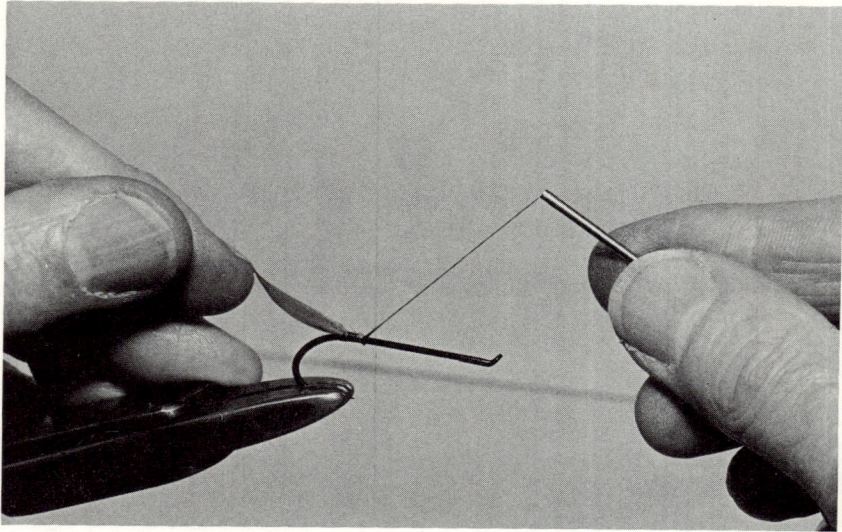

2
Make four turns of tying silk at the hook bend. With the tail cocked upward, center on top of the hook, and tie down. Close-wind the thread forward to ¼ inch from the eye of the hook. Coat the winding with head cement.

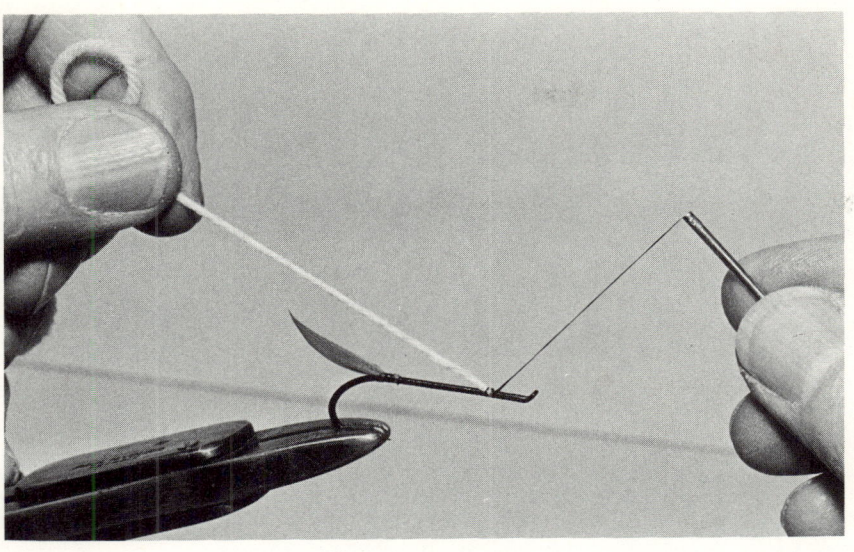

3
While the cement is still wet, tie in an 8-inch strand of white wool for an underbody.

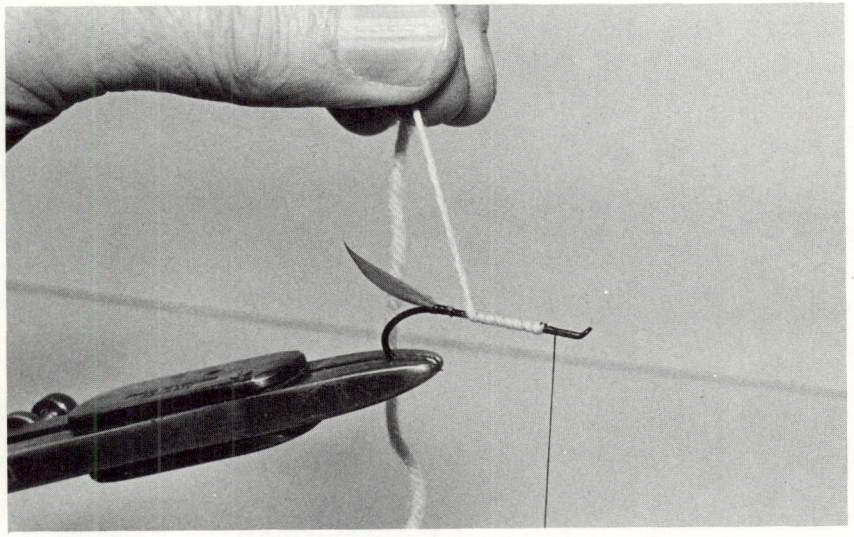

4
Wind the wool to the tail but do not cover the stub formed by the tied-down tail.

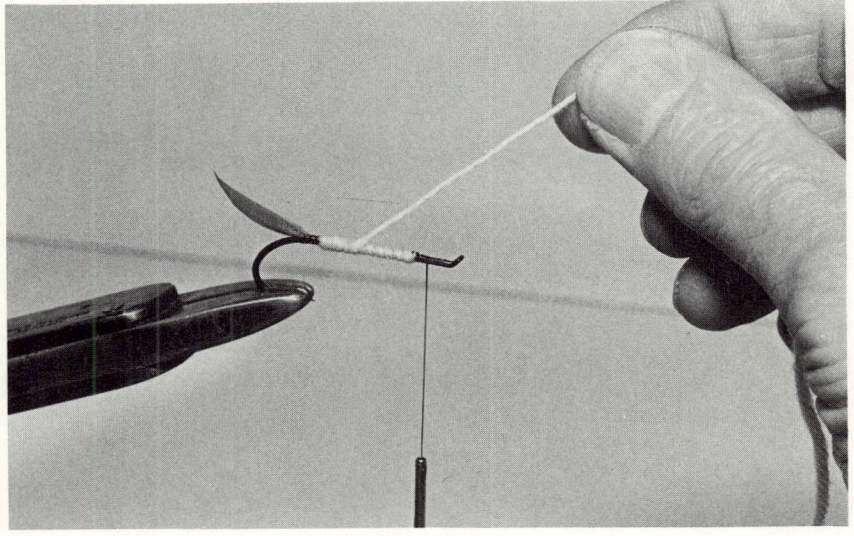

5
Keep pressure on the wool and tie over the first windings forward to head.

6

Tie in a 12-inch length of wide tinsel at the eye, covering the underbody. Keeping tight tension, wind to the tail, overlapping each wind slightly.

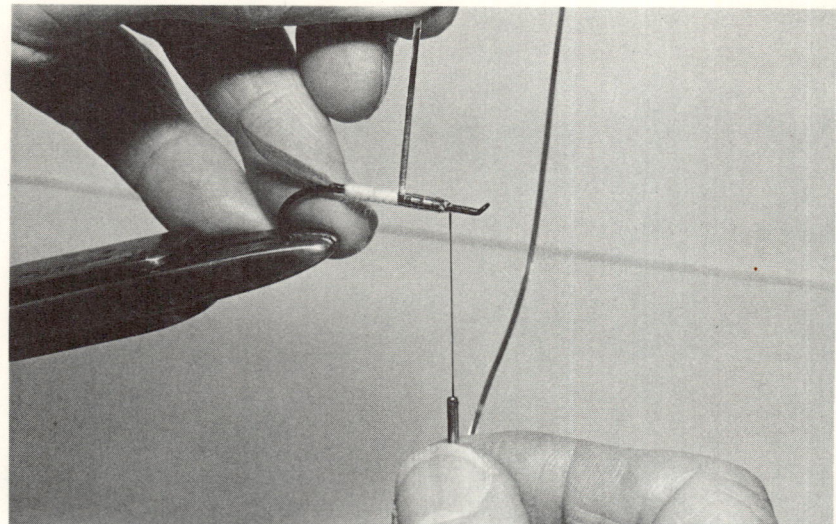

7

Wind the tinsel an extra couple of turns over the stub at the tail to bring it to the same height of body, then wind carefully back to the head. If the winds are not perfect, the white underbody is somewhat forgiving.

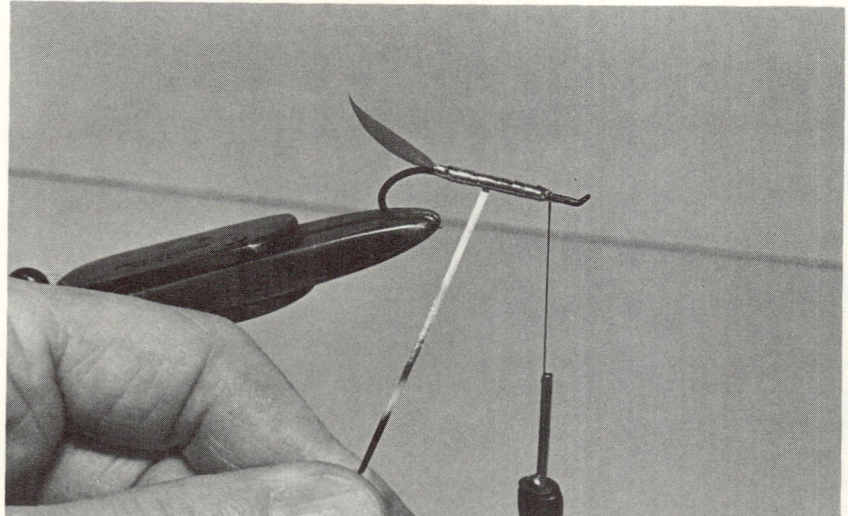

8

Cut a 12-inch strand of flat-red fluorescent floss. Dip a forefinger in head cement and run the strand between the forefinger and thumb to coat it thoroughly. Double the strand twice and cut the loops. Apply more cement and run the four 3-inch strands between the fingers again to make a single flat stripe approximately 1/32 inch wide.

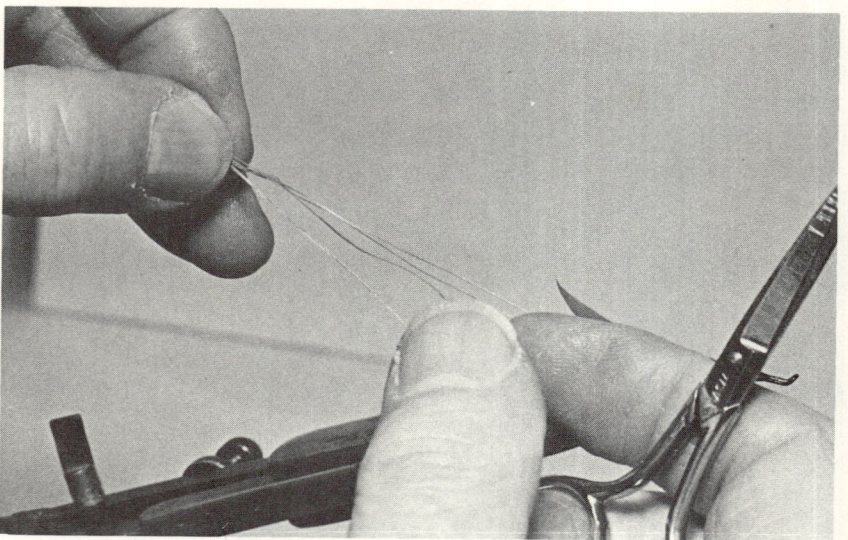

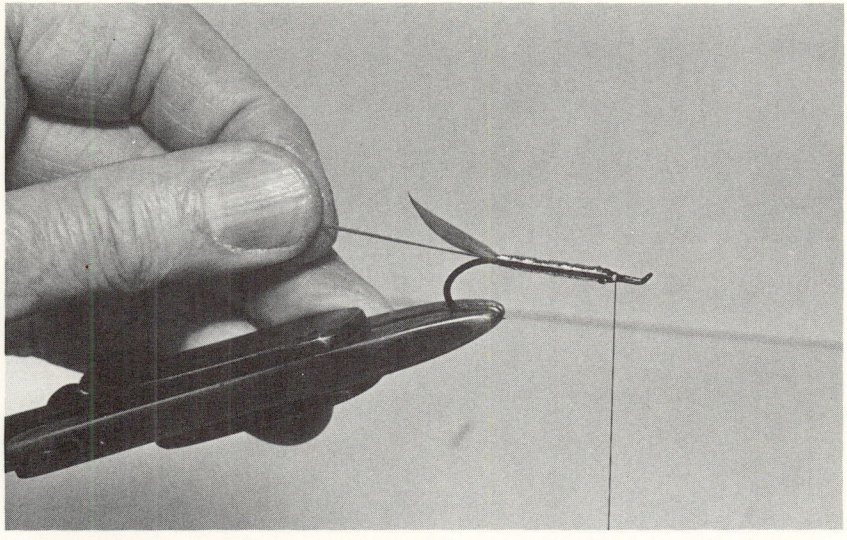

9

Tie in the stripe at the head of the fly. Put a dab of cement on the body, and while it is wet, lay the red stripe alongside the tail.

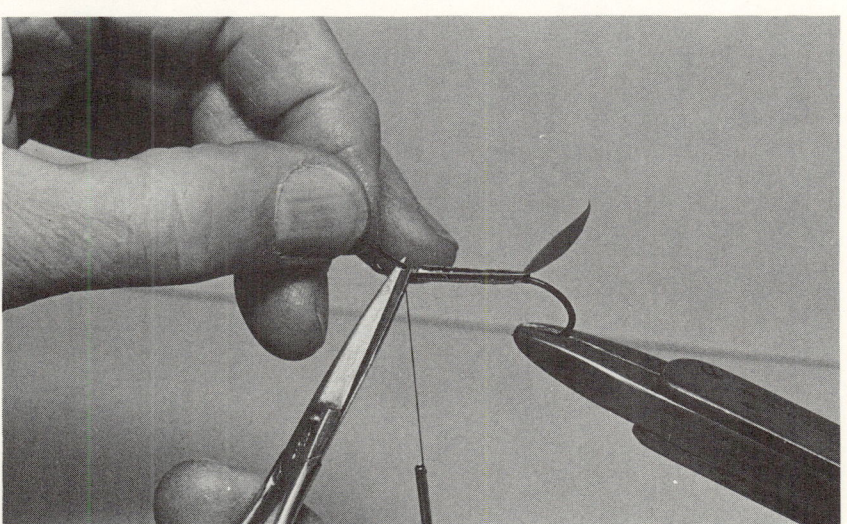

10

Continue the stripe along the far side of body to the head and tie off with a whip finish. Apply a coat of cement to the entire body and set aside to dry. Because of the need for drying time, it is more efficient to have several bodies in progress. I usually tie a dozen or so at a time.

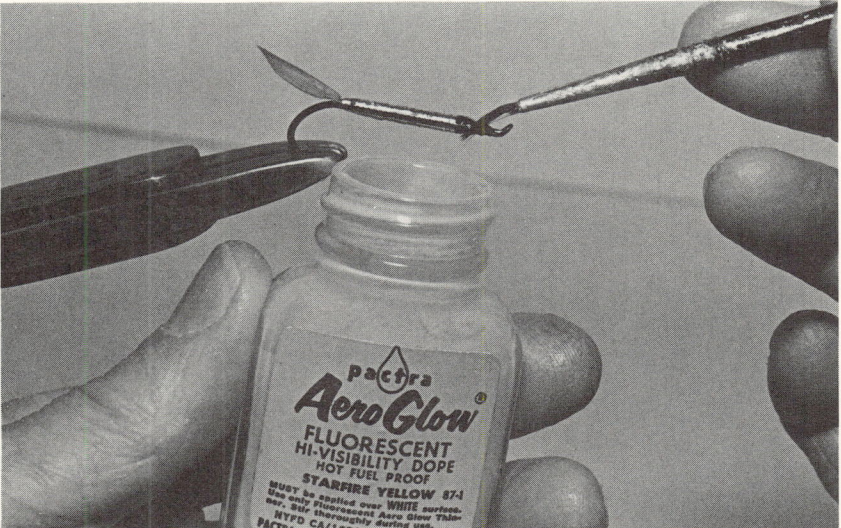

11

When it is thoroughly dry, paint top of the body between the two stripes with fluorescent yellow paint and set once more.

12

Two coats of paint are best, with a protective coat of cement on last.

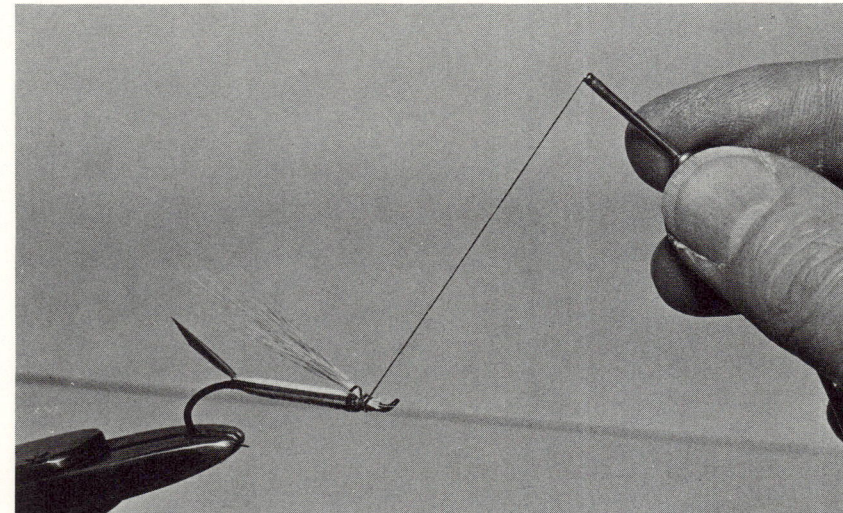

13

Tie in the underwing of yellow bucktail. Throw a loop around it before pulling it tight. This keeps the hair on top of the hook. Wrap several turns of thread over the butts.

14

Tie in a bunch of hot-orange bucktail for the overwing. The length should go to the tip of the tail. Again, put a loop around the bunch before tying it down.

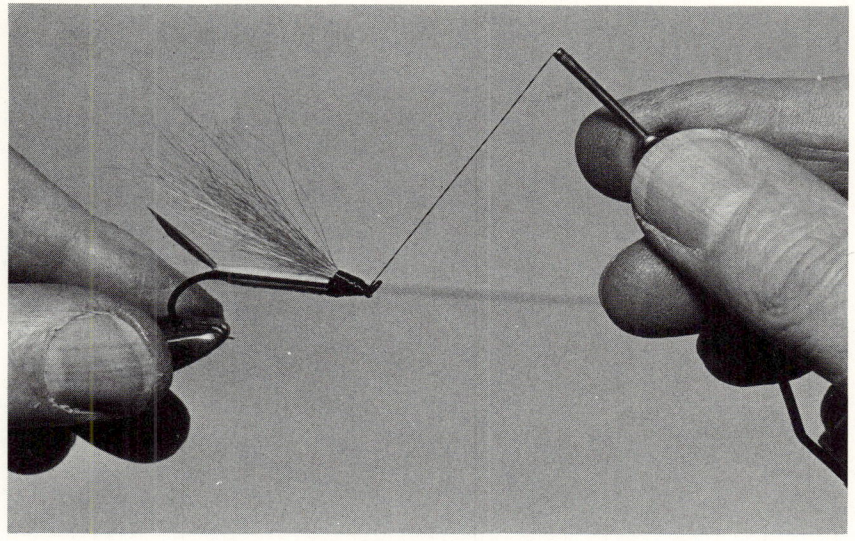

15
Build up the head with tying thread. Whip-finish and apply a coat of black dope as a base for the eyes.

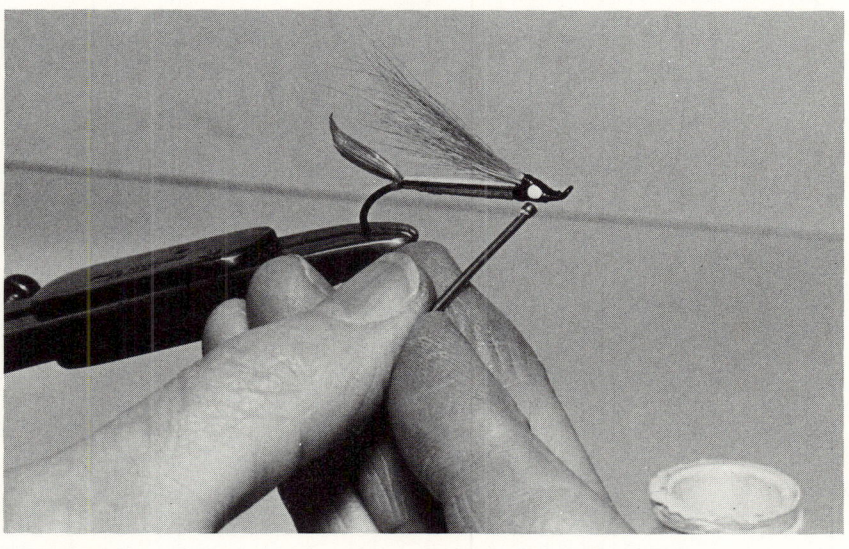

16
Put on the eyes with a finishing nail, the tip only dipped in white paint. Barely touch to the head to leave a single drop. Let dry.

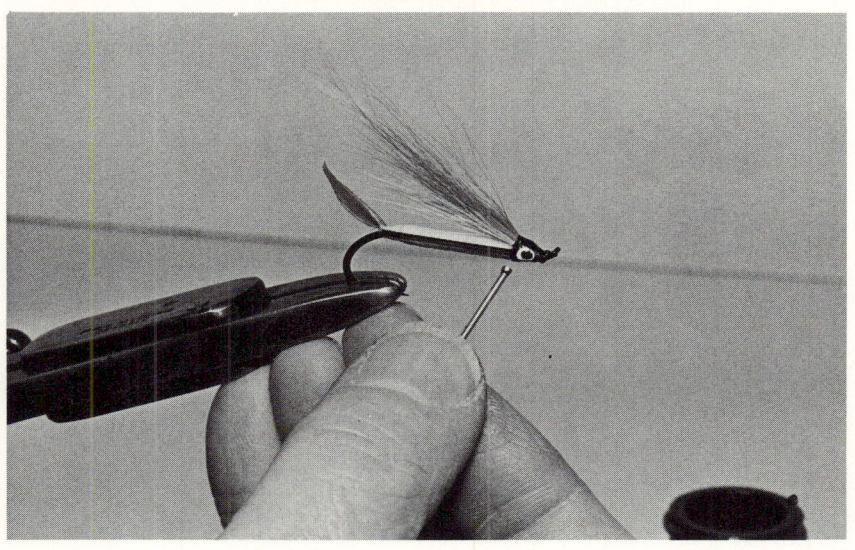

17
Apply black pupils with a smaller-size finishing nail, and the fly is complete.

Authors' Biographies

Walter Burr has been tying flies for over 30 years. At the University of Connecticut, where he was an assistant professor in the department of animal pathology, he conducted a student recreational fly-tying course for 20 years. Now an Emeritus Professor, he still teaches fly tying in retirement at Cape Cod, Mass. For many years he was the backbone of the United Fly Tyers organization, and served it as director. His writings in the UFT *Round Table* were prolific. He is a Colonel USAR (Ret.) and an active member of the USCG Auxiliary.

A professional fly tyer for four years, **Ted Godfrey** specializes in classic salmon flies. In addition to wholesaling and retailing of trout and salmon flies and fly framing, he has done some drawing and oil painting and has made split cane rods using the Kreider planing form method. His main haunts are the southern Pennsylvania limestones and freestone streams, with an occasional trip to the Catskills. Recently a frame of his flies was donated to the Museum of American Fly Fishing. He is associated with the Theodore Gordon Flyfishers and has participated as a director and angling arts writer for the D.C. chapter of Trout Unlimited. Married and with three children, Ted lives in Reisterstown, Md.

Ed Graham, a native of New York, began fly-fishing on the streams of the Catskill Mountains and has enthusiastically followed this pursuit ever since. His interest in fly tying coincided with his start in fly fishing, and has grown accordingly. As a conservationist, he has served as an officer of the Croton Watershed Chapter of Trout Unlimited for many years. He is a member of the Theodore Gordon Flyfishers, where he actively participated in the Water Quality Surveillance program. He is also a member of the Federation of Fly Fishermen and the American League of Anglers. An accountant, he resides in White Plains, N.Y.

  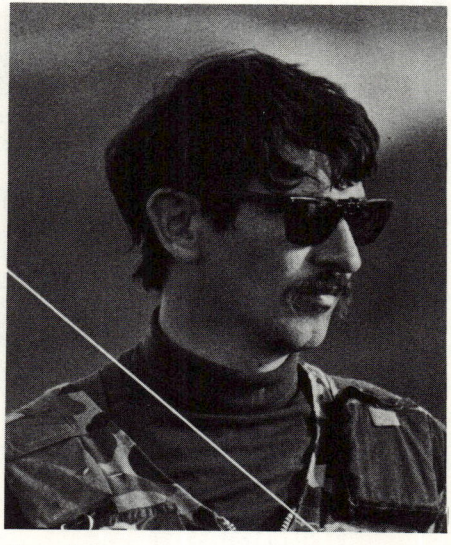

Hal W. Janssen is one of the West Coast's leading fly tyers. He has fly-fished extensively throughout the United States, Canada, Mexico, Alaska, and Costa Rica for just about every fresh and salt water game fish. A frequent winner in the annual *Field & Stream* fly fishing contest, he has been responsible for innovating a number of fresh and salt water flies. The Janssen Striper fly, the Bullhead, and the Half-Beak are some of his better-known patterns. His interest in fly tying has enabled him to become an expert on the subject of streamside entomology. Janssen is also an accomplished artist, writer, and speaker. His sketches appear in the *Anglers Calendar* and he has contributed articles to *Fly Fisherman* and *Angler* magazines. He is presently Sales Manager and Production Consultant for Sunset Line Co., located in Petaluma, Calif.

Charles Krom's love for creativity and the lure of the trout streams started him on his quest to learn the age-old art of fly tying. During several years of association with a well-known tackle shop in New York City, Charlie met some of the greats of the fly-fishing world, who had a profound influence on his style of tying. Today his work is sought after by fishermen and collectors alike, a tribute to twenty-four years of tying. Ten years ago, along with his wife, Loretta, and their three children, he moved to the peaceful hamlet of Highland Mills, N.Y., which is nestled between two old and great rod companies — a move he says was fate. When not fishing, Charlie earns his living as a professional firefighter in New York City.

Gary LaFontaine migrated from Connecticut to Montana as a university student and has lived there ever since. A professional fly tyer, he is credited with 34 original patterns in print. He is also a professional guide, photographer, and speaker at fishing clubs. His writings have appeared in *Field & Stream, Sports Afield, Fishing World, Fly Fisherman, Angler, The Flyfisher,* and *Flyfishing the West,* and he is a regular contributor to *The Fly Tyer*. Gary lives with his wife and daughter in Deer Lodge, Montana.

In more than 30 years of noncommercial fly tying, **Chauncey K. Lively** has originated many fly patterns and series including the Hair Carpenter Ant, Quill-Back Cricket, and the Golden Blazer Streamer. He also developed a unique method and a special tool for dressing bottom-parachute duns and bunched-parachute spinners, and assisted in developing and teaching a course in advanced fly tying, sponsored by Trout Unlimited. A regular columnist for the *Pennsylvania Angler*, he has also written on fly tying and fly fishing for *Trout, Fisherman's Digest, Outdoor People,* and *Angler's Annual* (England). His favorite fishing waters are Pennsylvania's limestone streams and the rich alkaline waters of Michigan's Lower Peninsula, and his hobbies include photography and stream entomology. In addition to serving on the board of the Penn's Woods Chapter of Trout Unlimited and United Fly Tyers, he is affiliated with the Federation of Fly Fishermen, Pittsburgh Fly Fisher's Club, Pennsylvania Outdoor Writers Association, Wilderness Society, and the National Wildlife Federation. A mortgage banker, he lives in Pittsburgh, Pa., with his wife Marion, also an avid angler.

John F. McKim was for many years a building designer, a career that left minimal time for family and fishing and, in 1966, accounted for a begrudged visit to the local hobby show with his young son, Mark. One exposure to the friendly fly tyers of the Long Beach Casting Club was enough to change his life. From student, instructor, and various club offices and activities to a directorship in the Federation of Fly Fishermen, his interest and enthusiasm has steadily grown. Two years as editor of the club's newsletter and four as editor of the *Tie Flyer* (where he signed himself "The Old Grouch") culminated in a new career, outdoor writing. His work is featured in various publications, including *The Flyfisher, The Salt Water Sportsman,* and *Western Outdoors,* where his column graphically illustrates the tying of a different fly pattern each month. John lives with his wife, Joanie, in Long Beach, Calif., where he is head of specifications for a consulting engineering firm.

John Merwin is the editor and publisher of *Rod and Reel*, a bimonthly magazine devoted to all aspects of American angling. He was formerly the managing editor of *Fly Fisherman* magazine, in which his articles and photographs on various aspects of fly tying appeared frequently. He lives in Dorset, Vt., and devotes much of his tying time to developing patterns for the fussy brown trout in the nearby Battenkill River.

S. A. Neff, Jr.'s 15-year pursuit of rising trout has taken him from the limestone-rich Henrys Fork in Idaho to the magnificent Gacka River in Yugoslavia. While living in Ireland, Sid developed a keen awareness of the traditions of fly tying. Although his fly designs are contemporary, the materials are traditional: silk, fur, and feathers. His flies have been exhibited at the Museum of Natural History, National Art Museum of Sport, and American Museum of Fly-Fishing, and are in many private collections. He has appeared in fishing films and has given angling presentations here and abroad. His tackle collection, spanning 150 years, and his fishing log observations, articles, and photographs provide him with a wealth of background on his subject. Sid lives in Pittsburgh, Pa.

A product of the Seattle area, **Ted Niemeyer** spent his early years fishing in the Northwest and Canada. There he developed an appetite for study and development of the exacting art of fly tying. But like all craftsmen, he continues to push on for better patterns, the desire to become a better fisherman providing the necessary incentive. Employed by United Airlines for more than 25 years, he has enjoyed the diversity of living in San Francisco, Chicago, Washington, D.C., Honolulu, and New York City. Presently the fly-tying editor of *Fly Fisherman* magazine, Ted has also done subjects for Art Flick's *Master Fly Tying Guide* and Alan Liu's *Sporting Collectors Handbook*. He is a member of the Federation of Fly Fisherman and on the advisory board of United Fly Tyers. He now lives in New Canaan, Conn., and with his wife, Phyllis, daughter, Laura, and son, Brad, enjoys the outdoors of New York, Vermont, and New Hampshire as well as annual treks to the Far West.

Eric Peper has been tying flies since 1969, having learned under the tutelage of Kenneth Bay at Theodore Gordon Flyfisher. He has been fly-fishing for 20 years all over the United States and Canada. His favorite fish is difficult brown trout in flat water; his favorite flies, those that are simple to tie, durable, and effective. Other hobbies include bird hunting, along with an appreciation for good fly rods and shotguns. He contributes the "Fly of the Month" column for *Field & Stream*, and has co-edited two books (with Jim Rikhoff) for Winchester Press: *Hunting Moments of Truth* and *Fishing Moments of Truth*. He is also founding editor of Field & Stream Book Club. Eric is employed by Control Data Corporation, Minneapolis, and lives with his wife, Norma, in Burnsville, Minn. They have three children, Anne, Susan, and Christopher.

John Shollenberger is a native of central Pennsylvania, where there is an abundance of fly tyers and fly fishermen. He started fly-fishing at the age of 14 and began to tie trout flies in the mid-1950s. He has given numerous fly-tying demonstrations in different states, and his flies are on exhibit in the Museum for American Fly Fishermen in Manchester, Vt., the William Penn Memorial Museum in Harrisburg, Pa., and the Federation of Fly Fishermen Traveling Museum out of El Segundo, Calif. In 1976 at the Federation of Fly Fishermen conclave in Sun Valley, Idaho, he won the Wayne Buszek Memorial Fly Tying Award and was awarded the gold feather pin. John is a member of the Federation of Fly Fishermen and Trout Unlimited. He lives in Tower City, Pa.

Dick Surette's forebears were Nova Scotia fishermen, and he was introduced by his father to the sport of saltwater angling off the coast of Cape Cod. His first love has always been flies, trout, and Atlantic salmon. The fly-tying bug bit at the age of 13, and a solid year of tying permitted him to trade off some flies for tackle. During his college years at Northeastern University in Boston, he exchanged a few odd dollars in the Commons until the authorities asserted that the main purpose of a university system was for educational and not fly tying endeavors. Finally in 1957 a degree was granted in Education followed by a teaching career of 15 years in New England and Europe. In 1965 he moved to the White Mountain National Forest in northern New Hampshire where, with an investment capital of $25, he opened a summer fly-tying business in a shed so small that only one customer could enter at a time. A few years later the foundation was laid for the Dick Surette Fly Fishing Shop, now open all year round with a mail order catalog as well. Among the original items to Dick's credit are the Riffle dry fly, the Latex Stonefly series, the *Trout and Salmon Fly Index*, and *How to Tie Basic Flies*. In May 1978 he started a new magazine, *Fly Tyer*, which he serves as editor/publisher, advertising manager, cover and layout designer, bookkeeper, and shipper. He lives in Mount Washington Valley, N.H., with his wife, Pat, four sons, and a daughter.

Ralph Wahl was born in the state of Washington, a short distance from the Skagit River, the state's premier winter steelhead stream. He started fly-fishing for steelhead in the early 1930s at a time when taking them by that method was not considered possible, and originated several successful attractor steelhead fly patterns that took fish to 20 pounds. Ralph is an active outdoors photographer specializing in black-and-white prints. His pictures have appeared in *Field & Stream*, *Sports Afield*, *Outdoor Life*, and other national and regional magazines, as well as newspapers and books. He has written magazine articles on fishing and photography and produced the photographic book *Come Wade the River*. A trustee of the American Museum of Fly Fishing and a director of the Flyfisher Foundation of Oregon, he is a past member of the board of directors of the Federation of Fly Fishermen and is currently active in three fly-fishing clubs.

Ralph was in the department store business for years before retiring in 1971. He still lives in Bellingham, Wash., his home base from which he periodically ventures forth to test the fly-fishing waters of his favorite Northwest.

Index

Adult Stone Fly, 75-83
   casting, 76
   materials, 77
   procedure, **77-83**
Alf, Dick, 47
Atlantic salmon, 102

Baetis nymph, 19
Barnes Special, 101
Bass, 101
Bates, Joe, *Streamer Fly Tying and Fishing,* 85
Beetles, 65
Bibios, 65
Bi-Fly, 75
Bird's Stonefly, 75
Black Chironomids, 67
Black Ghost, 101
Black gnat, 65, 67
Black midge, 93
Black Wulffs, 75
Blue Smelt, 102
Burr, Walter E., 1-4, **2-4,** 114
Burr's Brite, 1-4
   advantages, 1
   materials, 2, **2**
   procedure, **2-4**
   sizing wings, 1

Caddis flies, 65
Caddis Pupa, Emergent, 33-39, **34-39**
Cardinelle, 101-104
   materials, 102, 103
   procedure, **103-104**
Chiba, Bill, 102
Chironomids, 65, 67
Coho salmon, 102
Cotton-Thread Stonefly Nymph, 25-31
   materials, 26
   procedure, **26-31**
Covert, 65-66
Crayfish, feather-tied, 5-10
   materials, 6
   procedure, **6-10**
Crayfish, Ted's, 5-10, **6-10**
Creeks, 20

Damselflies, 41, 55
Deep Pupa, 33
Diptera, 93
Dragon Nymph, Marabou, 55-63, **57-63**
Dragonflies, 55
Dry fly, 1-4, **2-4**

Emergent Caddis Pupa, 33-39
   materials, 34
   procedure, **34-39**

Fan-wing, 1-4, **2-4**
Feather-tied crayfish, 5-10, **6-10**
Flat-Wing Caddis, 65-74, **68-74**

Flat-Wing Fly, 65-74
   materials, 68
   procedure, **68-74**
   wings, 66

Godfrey, Theodore J., 5-10, **6-10,** 114
Golden Blazer Streamer, 115
Graham, Edward, 11-17, **12-17,** 114
Graham, James, 11
Gray Ghost, 101
Green Ghost, 101
Grizzly Wulffs, 75

Hair Carpenter Ant, 115
Hair-tied crayfish, 5-10, **6-10**
Hair-Wing Matuka, 85-91
   materials, 87
   procedure, **87-91**
Halford, 65
"Hatch Master," 47
"Hatch, Salmon Fly," 75

Jane Craig, 101
Janssen, Hal W., 19-24, **21-24,** 116

Kreider method, 114
Krom, Charles, 25-31, **26-31,** 116
Kukonen, Paul, 102
Kusse, Ron, 25

LaFontaine, Gary, 33-39, **34-39,** 116
Lakes, 20
Lively, Chauncey, K., 41-46, **42-46,** 115

McKim, Joan, 47
McKim, John F., 47-53, **48-53,** 115
Marabou Dragon Nymph, 55-63
   materials, 57
   procedure, **57-63**
Marinaro, Vincent, 66
Matuka, Hair-Wing, 85-91
   materials, 87
   procedure, **87-91**
Matuka Sculpin, 11-17
   materials, 12
   procedure, **12-17**
May, Two-Feather, 47-53
   materials, 48
   procedure, **48-53**
Mayflies, 19
Merwin, John, 55-63, **57-63,** 75, 117
Michievicz, Jack, 5
Mickey Finn, 102
Midge, Vinny's 93-99
   materials, 94
   procedure, **94-99**
Mossback, 75
Mottram, J.C., 65

Nature flies, 75
Neff, Sid A., Jr., 65-74, **68-74,** 117

Niemeyer, Ted, 75-83, **77-83,** 117
Nine Three, 101
Northern pike, 102
Nymphs
   Cotton-Thread Stonefly, 25-31, **26-31**
   Marabou Dragon, 55-63, **57-63**
   Pre-Emerger, 19-24, **21-24**
Nymphs (Ernest Schwiebert), 56

Olmstead, James, 5

Painted Lady, 105-111
   materials, 106
   procedure, **106-111**
Parachute style, 47
Peper, Eric W., 85-91, **87-91**
Pike, 101
Pliobond, 66
Ponds, 20
Pre-Emerger Nymph, 19-24
   leg styles, 20
   materials, 21
   procedure, **21-24**
   tail, 19-20
   weighting, 19, 20
Pteronarcys Californica, 75
Pupa, Emergent Cadis, 33-39, **34-39**

Quill-Back Cricket, 115

Red Gray Ghost, 101-102
Rhodes, Bill, 19
Richards, Carl, 85
Ringrose, Dr. Vincent, 93-99, **94-99**
Rivers, 67
Robber flies, 41
Robber Fly, 41-46
   materials, 42
   procedure, **42-46**

Salmon, 101
"Salmon Fly Hatch," 75
Saunders, Bill, 33
Schwiebert, Ernest, *Nymphs,* 56
Scofield, Wilson B., 1
Sculpin fishing, 11
Sculpin, Matuka, 11-17
   materials, 12
   procedure, **12-17**
Shollenberger, John, 93-99, **94-99**
Smelt, 101
Sofa Pillow, 75
Sparkling Caddis Pupa, 33
"Spikes," 85
Stevens, Carrie, 101
Stickney, Joe, 101
Still-water mayfly nymph, 19
Stone flies, 65
Stone Fly, Adult, 75-83
   casting, 76
   materials, 77
   procedure, **77-83**
Stonefly Nymph, Cotton-Thread, 25-31, **26-31**

Streamer/bucktail flies, 101
Streamer Fly Tying and Fishing (Joe Bates), 85
Streams, 20
Striped bass, 102
Surette, Dick, 101-104, **103-104,** 118
Swisher, Doug, 85
Swope, Irv, 93

Ted's Crayfish, 5-10
   materials, 6
   procedure, **6-10**
Trolling patterns, 101-102

Trout, 5, 19, 25, 33, 41, 47, 55, 67, 75, 76, 102
Two-Feather May, 47-53
   materials, 48
   procedure, **48-53**

UFT Round Table, 1
United Fly Tyers, 1

Van Demark, Dick, 105-111, **106-111**
Vinny's Midge, 93-99
   materials, 94
   procedure, **94-99**

Wahl, Ralph, 105-111, **106-111,** 118
Wainwright, Andrew, 101
Walleyed pike, 102
Warden's Worry, 101
Welch, Herb, 101
Welch Rabbit, 101
West, Leonard, 65
Whitlock, Dave, 85
Winnipesaukee Smelt, 102
Wizard, 101
Wulffs, 75

Zander, Glen, 33